ATLANTIC CRUISE

Frontispiece: With bow and stern lines made fast to the royal palms, *Wanderer III* lies in the Kittredge lagoon at Fort Lauderdale, Florida.

ATLANTIC CRUISE IN WANDERER III

ERIC C. HISCOCK

Author of
Wandering Under Sail
Cruising Under Sail
Around the World in Wanderer III
Voyaging Under Sail
Beyond the West Horizon
Sou'West in Wanderer IV
Come Aboard

WITH 80 PHOTOGRAPHS
BY THE AUTHOR AND HIS WIFE
AND 7 CHARTS

ADLARD COLES LIMITED
8 Grafton Street, London W1

Adlard Coles Ltd
William Collins Sons & Co. Ltd
8 Grafton Street, London W1X 3LA

First published in Great Britain
in hardback by Oxford University Press 1968
Published in paperback by Adlard Coles Ltd 1987

British Library Cataloguing in Publication Data
Hiscock, Eric C.
Atlantic cruise in Wanderer III.
1. Yachts and yachting—Atlantic ocean
2. Atlantic ocean
I. Title
910'.09163 G465

ISBN 0-229-11747-3

Printed and bound in Great Britain

For

OUR AMERICAN FRIENDS

who made our visit to their country such a rewarding and enjoyable experience

ACKNOWLEDGEMENT

The acknowledgements of the author are due to the Editors of *Yachting* and *Yachting World*, in which magazines some parts of this story were first published.

CONTENTS

ILLUSTRATIONS

CHARTS

1

BISCAY

By the winter of 1964–5 the book about our last long voyage had been written and published; the film had been travelled and televised; and although we still had some lectures to give, Susan and I began to realize that we had used up most of the copy that had taken three years to collect, and unless we intended to give up voyaging and, like our neighbours, retire into our garden (then what would we live on apart from any vegetables we might grow?) we had better start planning a new venture.

'It seems absurd,' said Susan one morning as she poured our breakfast coffee, 'that we have never visited the United States. From what I have read it appears as though the east coast, and particularly the waterway part of it, might be fun; it's not all that far off, and if we cruised along it we could see a little of the country and meet some of the people.'

We had discussed this idea before when planning our second voyage round the world, but like others before us had reached the conclusion that it is almost impossible for a small sailing vessel going west-about from Europe to visit North America without extending the voyage by another year. This is a matter of winds and weather, and although a few small yachts have made westward Atlantic crossings in high latitudes to reach northern ports, a large proportion of strong headwinds can be expected on that route, together with some risk from fog and ice. Therefore the majority of voyagers, including ourselves, have preferred to take the southern route and sail by way of the north-east trade wind to the West Indies; but because of the hurricane season it is not wise to arrive there before November, and as January is the most suitable month for getting through the Panama Canal and out into the Pacific, one is tempted to continue on across the Caribbean without much delay. If, however, the intention is to cruise along the eastern seaboard of the United States, it is necessary to wait among the West Indies until May to avoid wintry weather before going north; then certainly that summer, and probably most of the autumn, would be spent cruising there, so that the transit of the Panama Canal would be postponed for nearly a year.

To make an Atlantic crossing specially to visit the U.S.A. seemed to us good sense, and many hours of that winter were spent on the living-room floor of our house studying charts and sailing directions. With a good fire burning in the grate while a winter wind bends the trees and rattles the windows, planning on paper is one of the cosiest occupations imaginable, and it is astonishing how far one can get in a single evening. I wrote to Bob Rimington, editor and publisher of the American magazine *Yachting*. We had never met—the meeting was something to which I could now look forward—but we had corresponded for twenty years and he had published some of my stories. I asked not so much for individual advice as for sources of information from which I could help myself; he told me of several books he thought we should have, and he gave us some valuable introductions. Americans do not respond to that kind of thing by halves, and soon we were receiving offers of information, help, and hospitality from people each of whom possessed wide knowledge of some part of the coast.

Wanderer III, our 30-foot sloop,* was now twelve years old, but although she had sailed a great distance we believed her to be in a condition fit to look after us just as well as she had done in the past. At the first sign of spring weather we removed her winter cover and started fitting her out, and for the forthcoming voyage we gave her several items of new equipment, notable among them being a windvane-operated steering gear, an echo-sounder, a bigger and better dinghy, and some stainless steel and Poole pottery for the galley.

* For technical details see *Beyond the West Horizon*, Appendix I.

Due to several misfortunes, including an injury to Susan's back, and to delays in the delivery of some items of equipment, we were later than we had intended getting ready for sea, and during the final few weeks when we were living on board in our home port of Yarmouth in the Isle of Wight, people in near-by yachts watched with some concern as twice a day Susan lay on her back on deck while I, apparently with sadistic intent, knelt on one of her shoulders and wrenched the opposite bent leg sideways. This, I hasten to add, was on medical advice in the hope of producing a click which might ease the trouble in her back. Our doctor, being a sailing man himself, understands small-boat people and their problems, and to save us some inconvenience had in the past often selected unlikely-seeming consulting rooms: in his car on the quay, or underneath the crane near the fuel-pumps, and once when with a pain in the starboard side of my abdomen I thought I had appendicitis, he examined me in the comparative seclusion of the yacht club boathouse.

Although the commencement of a long voyage in a small sailing vessel is not yet an everyday happening, it is not uncommon, and I sometimes wonder if the people concerned suffer from similar feelings to mine on such occasions: tense apprehension because of the knowledge that we will be dependent entirely on our own skill and resources, and a sad empty feeling at leaving behind the people and the things we love. I had hoped, as the years went by and I gained experience and a little more confidence in myself, that such feelings might become less strong; but I found on this departure in late June, when we slipped almost unnoticed from our home port, that I was just as apprehensive and just as sad as ever I had been before. However, a small sailing vessel can be relied upon to call for so much mental and physical agility that one cannot remain miserable for long, and soon it is not so much the immediate problems or the memories of what lies astern that matter, but the looking forward with keen anticipation to what lies ahead: the freedom, the progress, the landfall, the port, and the people—above all the people, for no matter how beautiful or how hideous a place

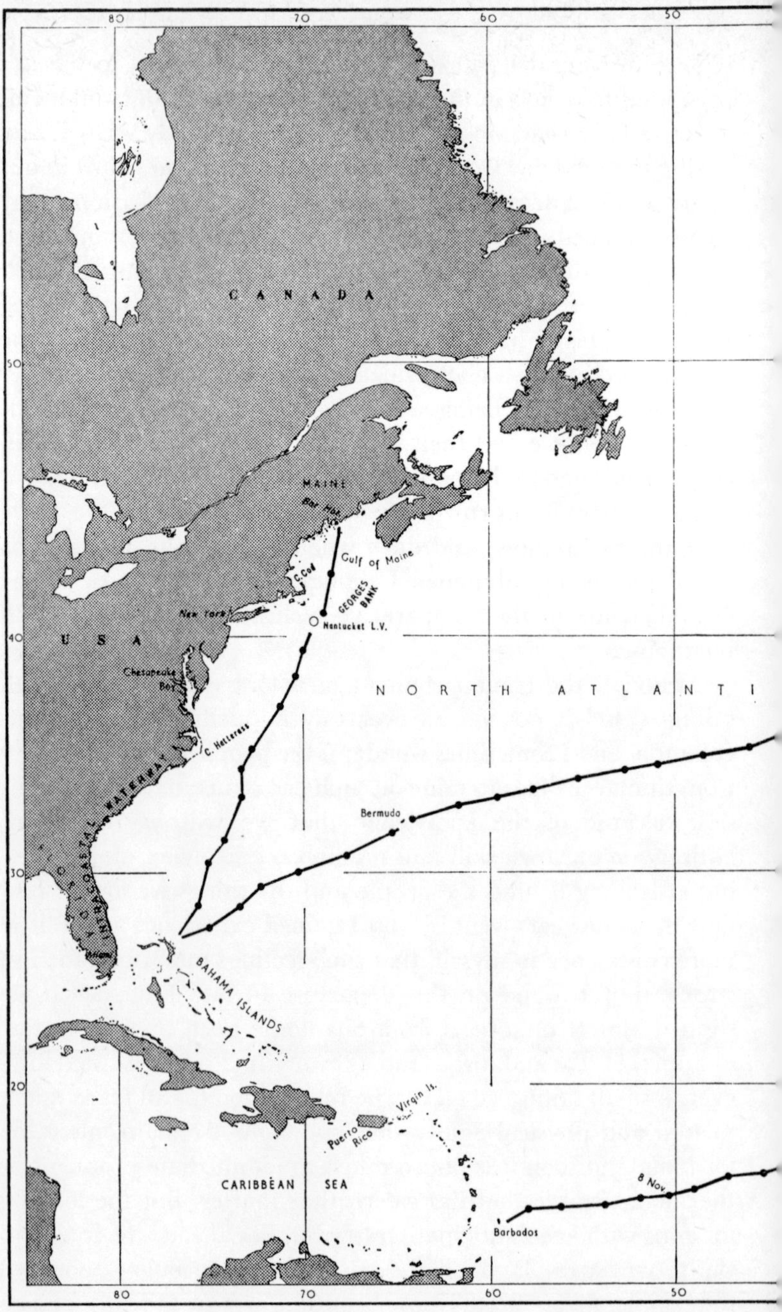

THE NO

For those areas where the track of *Wanderer III* is not s

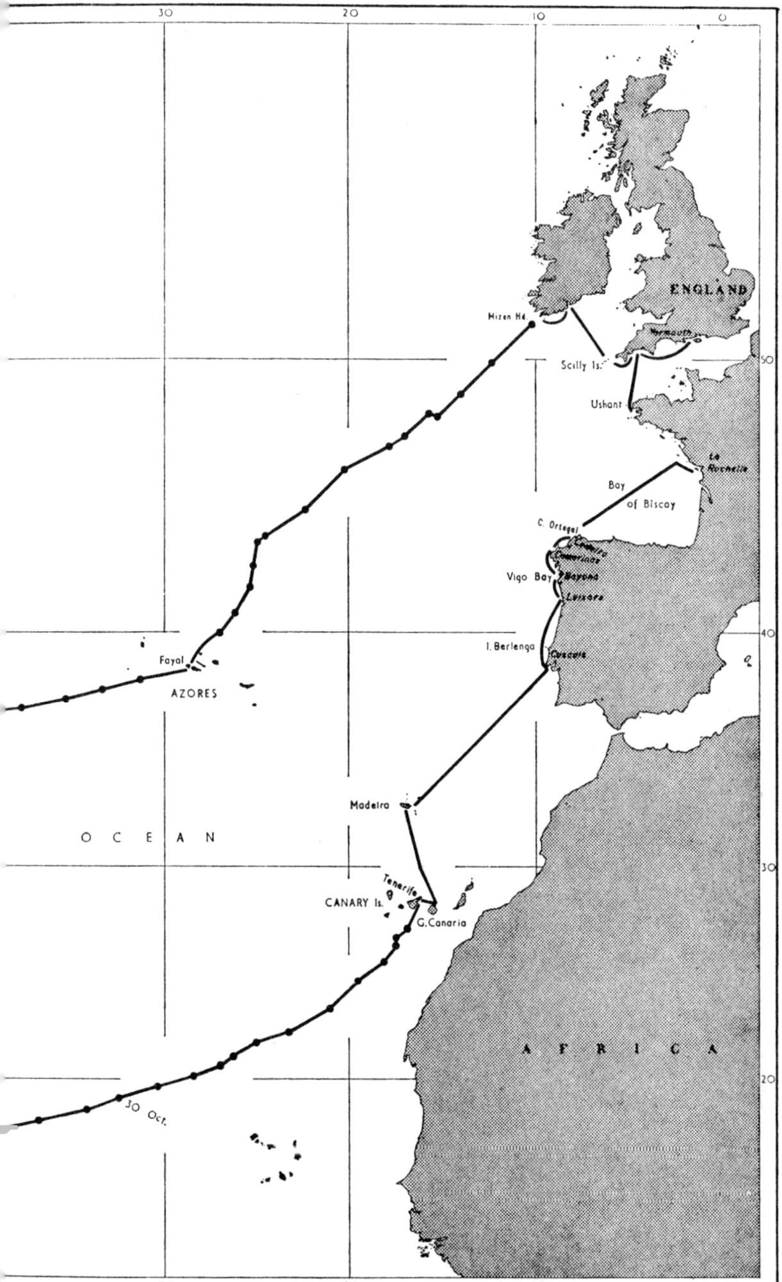

ANTIC

s of larger scale will be found in the relevant chapters

may be, it is the inhabitants who make it a worthwhile stop or a place to leave and forget as soon as possible.

Slowly a light breeze carried us down Channel and left us becalmed one morning before dawn near Ushant. That is an unhealthy place in which to drift about at the top of spring tides, so we started our motor and, as it was our intention to cruise for a little while along the south-west coast of Brittany, headed for the Chenal du Four, where the tall buoys surged by with bow-waves which suggested a speed of 6 or 7 knots. The swift stream hurried us through and shot us out at the southern end, where we picked up a breeze, and passing the entrance to Brest sailed pleasantly up the bay to the fishing port of Douarnenez. Since our last visit a new fishing-boat harbour had been built, and we sailed into it; but it had the grey, unfriendly atmosphere of a prison, so we turned away and brought up outside, fairly well sheltered from the wind by the harbour wall.

In response to our international 'Q' flag a harbour official came out with a simple form to be filled in, but did not wish to board us. New regulations for foreign yachts visiting France had recently come into force, but when we asked for the now-required 'passport for pleasure craft', much to our delight, for we mistrust bureaucracy, he denied all knowledge of it. We subsequently made twelve other stops in France, but at none of them was there any formality, nor were we visited or questioned by a single official. Such a civilized and easy-going attitude is surely to the benefit of everyone.

Our first stop in France is usually a pleasure, and this one at Douarnenez was no exception; the town could hardly be called attractive, but its people were smiling and helpful, and it smelt of fish, wine, the smoke of *Gauloises* and *pissat*. We shopped successfully, and returned aboard to gorge ourselves on an omelet, crusty new bread, strawberries and wine, and immediately fell asleep.

A disadvantage of Douarnenez is that it lies at the head of the bay, and it is a long haul out (17 miles) to reach the Raz de Sein, where it is essential to have a fair tide, and this meant a very early start. However, we were fortunate in having a fair wind to carry us down to and through the swirling Raz, but in the middle of Audierne Bay we realized that we were not going to save either our tide or our daylight round the next headland. So, as the wind was coming off the land, we closed with the shore and anchored off the village of Pors Poulhan, which in that largely built-over area we could not have recognized had its name not been painted in bold letters on the little lighthouse tower on the cliff. There is a bay, which dries and is used by a few small beach boats engaged in fishing when the weather is fine, and a short, high breakwater possibly gives some slight measure of protection to it, but our anchorage was quite open to the ocean. However, the weather appeared to be settled, so we landed on the breakwater to visit the village, and were shocked by the scene depicted on one of the postcards for sale, which showed a great sea breaking furiously right over the breakwater where we had left the dinghy, and across the bay.

We remained for the night, looking out now and then towards America, then gently sailed on to Loctudy, where, with wind and tide opposed, the pack of gregarious yachts looked so uncomfortable in the recognized anchorage off the town that we turned aside and found a quieter berth close to and just south of the jetty at Île Tudy.

It was at near-by Benodet that we first began to realize the size of the yachting explosion which had taken place in France, for there and at most of the other places we were to visit we found great numbers of yachts, mostly *plastique*; the majority of the small ones appeared to have no motors, and even with the large ones manoeuvring under sail was sometimes almost a fetish.

Before the war, when I was a single-hander, I visited the Belon river, which with its neighbour the Aven lies in attractive country between the ports of Concarneau and Lorient, and I believe my $4\frac{1}{2}$-ton cutter *Wanderer II* was the first British yacht to have called there. But today both it and the Aven are much used by yachts, and this time we chose to visit the latter. Having waited off the entrance for the tide to rise, as the river has a

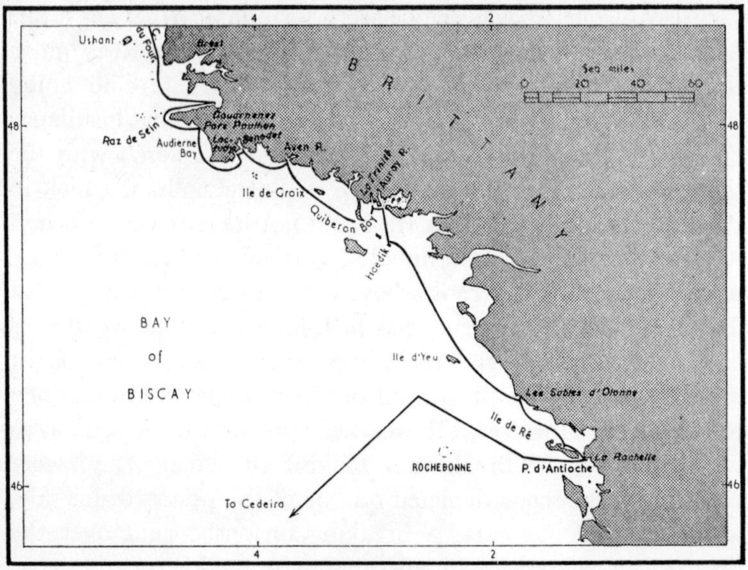

BAY OF BISCAY

drying bar, we found an anchorage in the pool one mile up it at Rosbras.

Until that year our dinghy had been an alloy 7-foot pram, and although this had served its purpose we sometimes thought, especially on rough, dark nights in open anchorages, that if anything caused us to drown it would probably be that little boat. So for this cruise we had replaced it with a 7½-foot dinghy of glass-reinforced plastics, a buoyant, stiff little boat with a nice round bow that does not splash. This made a great difference to our dinghy work, and excursions in it were a pleasure. During our stay at Rosbras, for example, needing money and provisions, neither of which could be obtained on the spot, we rowed in the rain 2 miles up the river and well beyond the boundary of the chart to the town of Pont Aven, navigating the wider stretches with the help of the sticks which mark the edges of the oyster beds, and guessing which branch to take when the ▶

1. The narrow entrance to St. Martin de Ré at low water.

river divided—we turned left there, and this proved to be correct. It was a pleasant expedition from which we returned damp, but full of fresh air and appetite, yet when that evening we met for the first time Norman Wates ('I am a bricklayer'—such modesty, for surely his must be one of the largest house-building firms in Britain), when he invited us aboard his yacht for a drink, and we told him about our little excursion, his comment was: 'Why, don't you have room for an outboard?'

A powerful north-west wind drove us along the coast at speed, past Île de Groix in a turbulent sea, through the Teignouse Passage into Quiberon Bay, and so, almost breathless, we came for one night to yacht-crowded La Trinité. Then on we went into the lovely Auray river, where oyster farming is the main industry; for miles both mud banks of the river at low-water mark are lined with the lime-coated tiles on which the oysters grow, and there is a busy movement of flat, black barges propelled by long sweeps attending to them, much of the work being done by sturdy women.

The Brittany coast and its islands down to this latitude certainly provides a jolly cruising ground, and although pilotage is intricate and the tidal streams run hard in some places, the dangers are so well and generously marked that in clear weather there is little need for anxiety. But the coast beyond was new to us, and, as we soon discovered when we started to do our homework on it, is comparatively lacking in good harbours where it is possible to lie afloat. Of these Les Sables d'Olonne was to be our first, and from the little island of Haedik, where we spent our last night in the Quiberon area, the distance is more than 70 miles. However, that tiresome local wind known as *vent solaire*, which after a quiet and sunny day gets up at about the same time as most people go to bed, drove us from our anchorage before dawn so that we managed to reach Les Sables before nightfall; but we spent such a wretched night there fending off our too-close neighbours each time a fishing vessel passed at

◄

2. The old port of La Rochelle is guarded by the fourteenth-century towers of St. Nicholas and La Chaine, seen here from the *avant port*.

speed, that we were glad to get out first thing in the morning and head for St. Martin de Ré, where there is a *bassin à flot*. As we approached the wind died, and we were just preparing to motor in when *Sulah Too*—we had already shared some anchorages and passages with this British 10-tonner—hailed and asked us to help, as her engine had broken down. We soon had her in tow, but progress was very slow, as our 8 h.p. engine was now moving a total of 18 tons, and as we passed in through the narrow, twisting entrance between high walls which excitingly hide what lies within, we wondered what we would find and we prayed that the gates to the *bassin* would be open, for with *Sulah* in tow we could not properly manoeuvre. Rounding a blind corner, we found that the gates were open, but, inexplicably, the low swing bridge above them was closed, and waiting to pass through was a bunch of small French yachts. Somehow we sorted ourselves out and tied up temporarily, and when the bridge did open there was a remarkable free-for-all as the yachts in a pack thrust through the bottleneck, some under sail (a little breeze had made by then), some under oars, and a few under power, and inevitably *Sulah* and *Wanderer* were carried in with them. But what a cosy feeling we had when the gates were closed and we knew that all must be peace until they opened at the next high tide.

The old fortified town of St. Martin de Ré, together with the harbour round which it clusters, is enclosed by a massive wall which appears still to be complete and in excellent repair, and as we relaxed and looked about us in the hot afternoon sunshine, we realized that we had now made some worthwhile southing; gone were the high-pitched grey slate roofs of northern France, their place being taken by low-pitched, almost flat roofs of red and orange tiles. That evening we were introduced to spider crabs for the first time when a Frenchman and his wife kindly invited us to dine with them at a restaurant specializing in *fruits de mer*. I am not skilful with crabs of any sort, but managed to extract all the meat that seemed worth bothering about in a few minutes, while our hosts took one and a half hours to do the job with absolute thoroughness; but, of course, dining out in France is regarded as a social just as much as a gastronomical occasion.

Looking down one morning from the battlements on to the narrow harbour entrance where an uneasy little sea was running, the wind being onshore, we witnessed a remarkable exhibition of seamanship, if one may call it that. A large yawl was attempting to beat out, and as the channel was in width little more than three times her length she scarcely stood a chance, and several times we felt anxious for her as she lost way and had to be pushed off with a boathook from one or other of the walls. Eventually she reached a situation from which it was clear no sail or boathook could extricate her. Her helmsman saw that, too; he pressed the starter switch beside him, a powerful but hitherto unsuspected engine sprang to life, and stern first with main and mizen full and drawing in the opposite direction she motored bravely seaward.

A disadvantage of wet docks is that one's time of entry or departure is ruled by the tide, for not until around high water can the gates be opened. On leaving we were bound for La Rochelle, where there is another *bassin à flot*, but as the time of high water there is the same as for St. Martin and the distance between the two ports is 11 miles, there is no possibility of leaving the one basin and getting into the other on the same tide. Therefore, on arrival at La Rochelle, the entrance to which lies narrow between the fourteenth-century towers of St. Nicholas and La Chaine, both of which are now floodlit by night, we naturally found the basin gates closed, so we tied up in the outer harbour alongside a French yacht of about our own size; she was tied up to a Luxemburg yacht which in turn was secured to a fishing vessel. As there was no wind and no tidal stream, I idly omitted to take lines to the shore, my excuse being that both quay and water were oily and I did not wish to soil the ropes unnecessarily; but I was soon to regret this. The owner of the Luxemburg yacht and his wife were having a drink with us aboard *Wanderer* when there was some shouting alongside, and a newly arrived yacht, travelling too fast, grabbed hold of us. The immediate result was that under the sudden strain our French neighbour's rotten bow line parted, and she with us and our hanger-on swung on her stern line and went foul of a fishing vessel next in line up the harbour, and we had to dismantle our steering vane in a hurry before it should get broken off under her flaring bow. Our guests helped us to sort out the mess and resume our original position, and to prevent the reoccurrence of such a happening I belatedly took a bow line to the quay. We had returned to our interrupted drink of Muscadet when I felt *Wanderer* heel and pivot, and on looking out found that the sluice gates astern of us had been opened, and this time the rush of water had parted the French yacht's rotten stern line, so that the pair of us had swung the other way on our bow line, and now with the French yacht, whose people had long since gone ashore for lunch, outside of us. While this pantomime was going on there was a constant and almost deafening roar from an unsilenced suction dredger at work close by. I thought just then that there is a lot to be said in favour of an open anchorage, even though one may have to clear out of it at dead of night. However, that evening we got ourselves into a safe berth in the *bassin* next to our old friend *Sulah Too*, whose merry company entertained us to a magnificent dinner ashore.

Like St. Martin de Ré, La Rochelle was overrun by trippers, gay young people attractively dressed, voluble and full of laughter; we enjoyed both it and them, and in particular the busy fish port which lay close to our berth. There deep-sea trawlers, returned from their fishing grounds, could be seen discharging their mixed catch into the wide acres of the fish market to be sold in a bedlam of echoing noise by auctioneers who carried amplifying equipment on their chests. Elsewhere ships were preparing for their next trips. Damaged wire cables were being long-spliced, and that was something I had supposed was done only in nautical textbooks; loads of crushed ice from great tip-up trucks were being shot down wooden chutes into the fish holds; welders, painters, shipwrights, engineers and electricians were busy at their jobs, and there was one humorist who momentarily silenced the ear-splitting racket of a set of pneumatic chipping hammers by grabbing the air-pipes and kinking them. By the lift bridge at high tide there were touching scenes of welcome from perfumed wives and sweethearts as the trawlers, rust-streaked and salt-stained from weeks of work on the fishing grounds, came in towards the dock; and there were even more moving scenes of farewell with tear-wet handkerchiefs, as the freshly painted outward-bounders turned their turtle-deck sterns to the women of La Rochelle and headed for the open sea.

Apart from moments such as these, France, as always, had been fun; but Susan and I felt that the real voyage for us had not properly begun until *Wanderer* had made her way down the long, narrow entrance channel, through the Pertuis d'Antioche, and out into the broad waters of the southern half of the Bay of Biscay, leaving behind the throngs of yachts and holiday-makers, bound for the more remote parts of Spain.

After a quiet start the wind came fresh from the west-south-west, a headwind for us, and as we stood away on the port tack, which was the least unfavourable one, we realized what we had already suspected—that via La Rochelle is no way to go to north-west Spain, for by visiting that place we had lost longitude to such an extent that we were back level with the Isle of Wight, and at that time of year west and south-west winds are common in Biscay.

Our first night out was most uncomfortable with a strong headwind and rough sea, and when just before dawn the Île d'Yeu light lifted above the horizon we knew that not only had we lost longitude by going to La Rochelle but now were losing latitude as well; however, at least we had avoided the Plateau de Rochebonne, on which there is a depth of less than three fathoms, and which is regarded by the *Bay of Biscay Pilot* as one of the most dangerous shoals off the French coast, for it is not exactly in its charted position, and the swell often breaks on it. Its edges are marked by four lighted buoys, but we passed too far to the north of it to sight any of these. With the rising sun the wind veered and moderated a bit, and putting about we were able to lay the course but progress was slow. Thereafter for much of the 330-mile passage to Cedeira we were hard on the wind, and we had some periods of calm.

As I have already said, for this voyage to America the ship had been fitted with a windvane-operated steering gear, so that we would not have to spend the long hours at the helm which had made our earlier voyages so exhausting, and as we have so often been asked how it works, perhaps a brief explanation here might not be out of place. The idea of using the wind to control the rudder and so keep a vessel on the desired course is not new, for such a device was used by the French single-hander Marin Marie as long ago as 1936 when crossing the Atlantic from west to east in the motor yacht *Arielle*, and nineteen years later the little sailing yacht *Buttercup*, owned by Ian Major, made a crossing in the opposite direction using such a contraption. Since then the need for self-steering gears by those taking part in the single-handed Atlantic races has led to developments and improvements, and such gears are now commonplace among the smaller ocean-voyaging yachts.

The general principle on which vane gears work is this: The yacht is put on the desired course and her sails are trimmed for that point of sailing; the vane, which is made of plywood or light metal, is then adjusted—often by means of a toothed wheel and latch—so that when the yacht is on her course it lies head to wind. If the yacht now goes off course the vane receives wind pressure on one or other of its sides so that it tries to turn head to wind again, and in so doing it moves the main rudder, an auxiliary rudder, or a trim tab, and thus brings her back to her course, when the vane once more lies head to wind. The gear we had in *Wanderer III* was of the trim tab type, i.e. a small hinged flap (the trim tab), controlled by the windvane, was fitted to the trailing edge of the rudder. When this tab is turned in one direction it imparts, because of its advantageous position and the water flowing past it, a considerable turning force to the main rudder in the opposite direction. So, when the yacht wanders off course the wind turns the vane, the vane turns the tab, and the tab turns the rudder. The biggest problem to be overcome is the provision of a vane of efficient shape and sufficient area, requirements that are usually restricted by the position of the end of the boom in relation to the permanent backstay or other essential gear, and often the only way to get sufficient area is to make the vane tall and narrow, but then it is not possible to support it very well.

Colonel H. G. (Blondie) Hasler, the originator of the single-handed Atlantic races and an active participant in them, has made a close study of vane-gear requirements, and is now widely regarded as a leader in this field. He is also a personal friend of ours, so it was natural that we should fit one of the gears that he had devised, and affectionately call it Blondie. During trials in the Solent with Hasler and his partner, Major Jock McLeod (who had crewed for the Pyes on their cruise to South America in *Moonraker*), on board, it became clear that in certain circumstances the vane was not large enough to move the tab, and it had to be enlarged in the only possible way by increasing its height; this caused it to shake angrily in strong winds when idling. But because of lack of wind or proximity to the shore or to other vessels, we had not had much opportunity until now of trying it out for any length of time, and we found that it worked splendidly. Once the correct setting for the latch on the toothed wheel had been found, the helmsman had nothing to do but watch fascinated as the vane moved the rudder one way or the other to correct any tendency of the ship to wander off her course; and it was soon obvious that the vane made a better job of steering than a human helmsman could, for it never let its attention wander. It was quite wonderful to be able to move about freely and to keep a look-out from the dry security of the companionway instead of from the spray-showered cockpit, and in between whiles to read a book. But this was not a proper test for the vane gear, because *Wanderer* is well balanced and easy to steer when the wind is forward of the beam, and later on we were to discover that there were circumstances in which it could not manage without a little help, but these were rare.

Early one morning when we were within sight of a dozen white lights, which we took to be those of a fishing fleet, the wind died right away, so we put up our own riding light and turned in. As dawn crept over the pewter sea the white lights faded to reveal that each belonged to a gaily painted Spanish tuna-fishing vessel with flaring bows and tremendous sheer. When they got under way each made a high-speed circle round us, the large crew waving enthusiastically, then, with the long slender fishing rods outstretched on either side, hurried off about her proper business.

During the late afternoon of our fifth day at sea we sighted the high land around Cape Ortegal, Spain's northern point. The wind, which as before had been allowing us just to lay the course, then backed, and all through the night we beat wetly to windward to round the apparently never-ending bulge of land, fixing our position now and then by bearings of the lights on Punta Estaca (25 miles visibility) and Punta Candelaria (22 miles). Susan was on watch at dawn, and she was careful not to lose the position of the latter light when it was extinguished, for on that strange, high and misty coast it was our only sure clue to the whereabouts of our intended destination, the Ria de Cedeira. As the daylight of that heavily overcast morning reluctantly increased, there the lighthouse still was, a tiny white speck high up the frowning grey face of its headland. We steered to leave it to port, and as we closed with the forbidding shore the north-west swell, which is the curse of this coast just as it is of so much of the North Atlantic, began to lose height, and soon after breakfast we sailed in smooth water in among the blue-green hills which cradle the Ria. As we did so the clouds vanished as though by magic, and rounding the point where the big cannon rust in the grass, we entered the anchorage where the local fishing boats lay on moorings, a golden beach behind them, and on the steep hillside overlooking it hung small fields and gardens with their crops of potatoes, maize, beans, and cabbage. At the quay an ancient wooden steamer was loading pit-props, and a pleasant smell of wood smoke from the bright little town hung on the air.

▶

3. *Top:* The fish market at La Rochelle, where the catch is auctioned in a bedlam of echoing noise. *Bottom:* The fruit and vegetable markets of Spain also are full of life and noise.

2

IBERIA

I have often thought it a mistake to repeat something which has been enjoyable, for fear of disappointment, but this our fourth visit to Spain in fifteen years proved me wrong, and Susan and I enjoyed the people and the country more than ever. Visiting yachts, though still comparatively few, are no longer regarded as curiosities to be stared at, and their people when ashore are not followed about by hordes of wide-eyed children such as on our first visit almost scared us away from some of the more remote places. Apart from the occasional visits of port officials or the *guardia civilia*, who come more out of curiosity than for any other reason, there are few formalities, but this may not be so in southern Spain, where smuggling by so-called British yachts does create difficulties. Ashore we found nothing but civility and honesty and a readiness to help in any way possible. This may have been due partly to the fact that Susan had learnt a little Spanish during the previous winter, and her attempts at pronunciation were often the cause of much amusement; sometimes in places where she had become known through frequent visits to the shops or market, her appearance was the signal for a small crowd to collect and join in the fun with smiling attempts to correct her.

We particularly enjoyed Cedeira, not so much for its beauty or its clean, well-sheltered anchorage, but because it was so busy with its proper business of exporting pit-props, fishing, and market gardening; and its people, who clearly were not

◀

4. *Left:* The old town of Cedeira on the north-west coast of Spain, where, *right,* the shopkeepers made smiling attempts to correct Susan's pronunciation of their language.

accustomed to having many visitors, for the place is out on a limb, treated us more as guests and gave the impression that they enjoyed our company. The shopkeepers went to much trouble to understand our wants and then provide them, or find someone who could do so, and when one day we were on the hillside overlooking the anchorage and asked some women who were harvesting potatoes the way to the cemetery, one of them, quite elderly and with a basket of potatoes on her head, led us to it and, burdened though she was, tried to help Susan over a stile; when we returned later to film them at work, they insisted on giving us a present of potatoes. Incidentally, it seemed that space in that cemetery was limited, the coffins being placed not underground and individually, but closely side by side in a system of partitioned shelving, each with a narrow ledge outside for the occasional flower. The jovial Captain of the Port and I, although we could not converse, became *amigos*, and every time we met there was much back-slapping and laughter, and sometimes he accompanied me with an arm around my shoulders.

We were on the coast of Galicia for most of August, a period of unusual and almost complete calm, and although we made some use of such faint airs as there were from time to time, mostly we had to motor in glassy calm to make any worthwhile progress. The majority of the places at which we stopped had been visited by us before, but the port of Lage was fresh to us, and there we nosed in behind the sturdy breakwater and anchored where a fisherman indicated. It was a tight berth, and we seemed to be much in the way of the fishing vessels and coasters which came and went throughout the night, but there, as in other busy ports of Spain and Portugal, nobody seemed to mind, and the vessels were handled with such skill and lack of fuss that after an hour or two we no longer felt too vulnerable.

At Lage we met *Northern Light*, the big gaff ketch which is the home of the Griffin family and in which they were sailing from Poole towards Nassau. An attractive picture her long, varnished dinghy made returning under oars from the shore that evening, carrying Jimmy and Anne and their four daughters, whose uniform was white jeans and white shirts with the ship's name embroidered on them.

Next day in the continuing calm we motored on, rounded Cabo Villano (the villain) in poor visibility with a threat of fog, and with some concentrated use of sextant and hand bearing-compass, found our way through the inshore channel to Camariñas to buy fuel, which had not been obtainable at Lage, and there endured a day of heavy rain which washed sardine oil out of the fish factory ashore and thinly coated the *ria* with it. Then on along the lovely mountainous coast we plodded our slow way, our only excitements being those incidental to pilotage, for none of the many off-lying dangers are marked except perhaps by breakers, and the only way of fixing one's position is by bearings or angles of distant mountain peaks, which are not always easy to see or identify. Eventually we reached Vigo Bay, spent a night off Cangas on the northern shore, one of swelling Vigo's dormitories, and then slipped across to the little basin which lies beside the Real Club Nautico de Vigo, where mail should be waiting for us, and we could conveniently fill up with fuel and water.

We had intended to stop there only long enough to do those things, for the basin is unclean, but as we were making our way up the gracious stairway of the club to the secretary's office we were accosted by a member who introduced himself as Dr. Ruiz. He appeared to be expecting us, and told us that the Commodore, José Masso, wished us to lunch with him in the club that day. This altered our plans a little. We hurried back to *Wanderer* to get properly dressed, and while doing so were boarded by Fernando Solano, a genial man who spoke American almost as his native tongue. He, too, wished to entertain us, and hurried plans were made for a longer meeting at Bayona in a few days' time. Lunch, a tremendous meal, was served on what one might perhaps call the 'shelter deck', the club house being designed something on the lines of a passenger ship complete with funnel, and with the stern alongside the basin and pointing to the sea; as we sat our eyes were level with *Wanderer*'s gilded truck, and Susan whispered to me, 'What a blessing we put up a new burgee today!' Conversation was not easy because of the language barrier, but there were little presents for us: a brooch for Susan bearing the insignia carried by all of José's ships (he owned not only the fish factories at Cangas and elsewhere, but fleets of trawlers and whaling ships) and for me a mounted silver scallop, 1965 being the year of the scallop at Santiago de Compostela.

Full of good food and excellent wine, and with a comfortable feeling of being for the moment important, we made our way down to *Wanderer* lying in the basin below, had a slight misunderstanding between us as to the best procedure for turning and getting out of that tiny place, and then in hot sunshine but with a pleasant little breeze, sailed our sleepy and contented way up through the fleet of more than a hundred mussel-growing rafts (these may now be found in many Spanish bays, and as they show no lights can be a hazard after dark) to the Ensenada de San Simon, a pool 2 miles in diameter at the head of Vigo Bay, where we bathed, cleaned up, and read our mail.

A day later, as we were sailing down the bay to rendezvous with Fernando, we saw jilling about off Vigo the British yacht *Valfreya*. John and Jane Cordiner with their son Jonathan had wintered in her at our home port, and now, making their first voyage, were bound towards New Zealand, where they intended to settle, and were carrying most of their possessions along with them. They had just arrived off their first Spanish harbour six days out from Loctudy in Brittany, and quite understandably were a little bewildered and could not see the way in. We were able to point out the concealed entrance to the basin, and then sailed on for Bayona, entering by the Canal de la Porta, the short cut inside the row of little islands where, unusual in Spanish waters, the tide runs hard. There the wind left us, and the motor, which recently had developed a rattle that I could not trace, but feared was going to prove expensive, had to take us into the anchorage, where we let go close to the bathing beach under the high ramparts of Monte Real, secure from any wind that might blow. That night we lay in dark water so calm that the stars were reflected motionless in it, while all around was soft talk and an occasional snatch of opera as the night fishermen, in their big pram-ended dories, jigged for squid, which is one of the most popular dishes in Spain.

We knew from earlier experiences that Bayona provides the last clean and snug anchorage for a small yacht this side of the Atlantic, and we made the most of it. Daily we landed, not on the bathing beach—this, remarkably, was cut off from the rest of Spain by water and the unscalable castle wall, and was reached by the many holiday-makers in ferry boats under oars, each of which carried a faded Spanish flag, its staff thrust into a rowlock socket—but on the south-west beach of firm sand, which was used by the fishermen for scrubbing and painting their vessels, and on which the crew of *Pinta* (Columbus's consort) landed on their return from the New World, and did our simple shopping in the nice old town. While we were in Spain our lunch always consisted of bread and cheese, wine, and grapes, and the grapes we bought in Bayona far exceeded in flavour and sweetness any we had previously tasted.

We were told of plans for building a yacht marina at Monte Real, when the bathing beach would no longer be available to the public, the intention being to encourage more foreign yachts to visit the area (that year 130 went to Vigo Bay). In opposition to such a scheme, which might so easily spoil the place, I offered the opinion that the cruising man's requirements are generally quite simple; a quiet, clean anchorage, a safe place at which to land and leave the dinghy unmolested, and a near-by tap at which water containers can be filled, are surely the essentials, and to these one might perhaps add a fuelling point. The first requirement Bayona already provides admirably, and it is something so precious that nothing should be allowed to interfere with it. The second and third could be provided at very little cost by building a short jetty out from the wall half-way along the town's waterfront.

Notwithstanding my opposition to their scheme, our Spanish friends were most kind. Dr. Ruiz and his wife took us by outboard under the Roman bridge and up the winding Rio Miñor among the fields and houses and paddling children, until weed repeatedly fouling the propeller stopped further progress. Fernando took us with Commodore José Masso for a 100-mile drive to see the sights of the Rias Bajas (Vigo, Pontevedra, and Arosa, all of which we had cruised in) from the land. It was one of those jolly occasions one remembers for a long time. José and Fernando chattering away in front (Fernando translating for our benefit), José now and then egging Fernando on to greater speed, but Fernando, we were thankful to note, was not to be hurried that day. We visited the vast sardine factory off which we had anchored a few nights before at Cangas, to watch 500 girls putting the fish into cans, and José tried to obtain samples of his products for us. But although he was the owner, this was apparently none too easy, and finally he said:

'Well, never mind; I have more factories.'

So we drove on to Bueu, a town on the south shore of Pontevedra Bay, of which he had been mayor for twenty-five years; here he had better luck, and obtained for us some cans of remarkably tasty smoked sardines (to the astonishment of the waiters he opened one of these at the restaurant to which he took us for lunch so that we might sample the fish), tuna, and 'octopus stuffed and packed in its own ink'. We visited his family's remarkable nautical museum, which is not normally open to the public, but anyone who can discover its whereabouts and the keeper of the key is welcome to look round, and there will find some rare and valuable manuscripts, charts, and models, which I fancy the National Maritime Museum at Greenwich might be very glad to have. Then on and on we went, one magnificent vista succeeding another, while all below lay the quiet, blue and shining sea.

At dawn one morning towards the end of August we motored seaward, and a mile or two offshore thankfully picked up the first real wind we had had in a month, and that was to be the end of motoring for many a day. How good it was to see the mainsail and spinnaker hard-curved and full of wind, to hear the roar of the bow-wave and watch the broad wake streaming astern as we ran steadily to the south!

The last Spanish port before reaching the Portuguese frontier is La Guardia, an exciting place with black and colour-washed houses piled steeply up around its rocky cove in which a fleet of fishing vessels lay pitching in the swell, for it is open to the ocean and certainly was no place for us. So we continued on our way down the straight and featureless coast, heading for the artificial harbour of Leixoes (the port for the city of Porto) and for several miles were in close company with an old, coal-burning trawler, whose speed was the same as ours. As we passed the tall Leca lighthouse in the late afternoon and saw the harbour walls ahead, the sardine fleet was just putting to sea, and having once before entered while the fleet was leaving, we had no wish to repeat the experience, so we shortened sail and waited until we thought most of the vessels were out. But we had not reckoned with their number, and subsequently learnt that 180 of these big craft, each with a crew of forty men or more, put to sea each evening except on Saturdays from April until the following January. As we rounded the end of the outer, sunken breakwater and, close-hauled, anxiously fetched in towards the blind corner made by the eastern wall, many more came roaring out. Our deck was sluiced by their steep wash, spray rattled on our sails, and we were indeed thankful to come at last into the sheltered inner harbour, where a red-coated boy from the Clube de Vela Atlantico was waiting by the only vacant mooring, to which he helped us secure.

I have in the past been criticized for things I have written about Portugal's 'international' policemen. Some of these remarks appeared in one of my books, and I was embarrassed when the then Portuguese Ambassador in London, owner of the fine schooner *Bellatrix*, bought a copy at one of the boat shows at which *Wanderer* was an exhibit, and asked me to autograph it. Later I received a charming note from him together with a printed copy of the revised rules for the treatment of foreign yachts. His note concluded with the hope that Susan and I would visit Portugal again one day. This we did, but only to discover that the policemen had apparently not yet heard about the new rules, and they treated us just as harshly as before. However, on this our third visit we found a different attitude.

A few minutes after our arrival we were boarded by a courteous official; he welcomed us to the port, invited us to make full use of the club's facilities, and asked me to sign a green card. Next day he returned the card, which had been stamped by the port, police, health and customs authorities, and this was the yacht's passport, which we might be asked to show in other Portuguese ports. He did not ask to see our personal passports. I would never have presumed to claim that the change was in any way due to what I had written but several people assured me that this was so.

We had not meant to linger at Leixoes, but several days of fog induced us to do so. Whether the fog was a local phenomenon I do not know, but it did not stop the movement of shipping. One afternoon from the end of the inner harbour wall we could just make out the blurred shape of a slowly moving outward-bound freighter, and hard in her wake could see a shoal of sardiners—where she could go so could they, and in the event of a collision no doubt she would serve as a useful buffer. From the wide sand beach at the north side of the harbour a rickety wooden staging had been built leading to the top of the 50-foot-high wall, and there three women were at work. One was filling baskets with sand and placing them in turn on the heads of the others who, slowly and almost painfully it seemed, then made their way up the steep incline to empty their loads over the wall, but for what purpose we could not guess. The scene might have been set in the heart of some desert a thousand years ago; the beach gleamed almost white in the intense light, but all beyond a limited circle was dimmed or masked by the fog. On that same beach not 100 yards away stood row upon row of beach tents like soldiers on parade: there the idle, the wealthy, and the holiday-makers were disporting their bronze bodies in a modicum of beachwear, and there was a coming and going of pinafored maids with picnic baskets and ice-boxes on their heads.

▶

5. Our 30-foot sloop *Wanderer III* had already carried us some 90,000 miles when she set out on her voyage to America. Designed by Laurent Giles and built by William King, she can set a total of 600 square feet of sail.

Our way back to the grey stone box in which *Wanderer* lay imprisoned by the fog took us through the long, cool, cathedral-like boathouse of the club. Outside crouched a scarlet two-seater Jaguar, and within, ranged each side on their neat trailers, stood two rows of polished and immaculate speed-boats. And all that day and for several days the Leca siren, its blast finishing on a high note like a question mark, roared its warning over the shrouded scene; and there were other sirens from ships groping, and over all the damp feel of spume and the dull boom of surf. Daily the women continued to dig and carry sand.

Then at noon one day the Portuguese trade wind, the strong northerly which is a feature of this coast, suddenly resumed business; in a matter of minutes it blew the fog away and cleared the harbour of the oil that had collected there, and the sun shone. We had a quick wash down, and in company with *Dido*, the tiny yacht in which Bill Buzzard and John Bennet (young but redundant draughtsmen from an aeroplane factory) had sailed out direct from Bristol, and were now heading for Madeira and beyond, left the harbour and found the wind strong and the sea rough outside. *Dido* stood away offshore, while we under reefed mainsail and small spinnaker headed for Ilha Berlenga (Burling Island) with the idea of calling there if conditions were suitable. It was fast going, and we had to reduce sail at nightfall as the wind continued to increase and the sea to build up. We sighted Mondego, one of the powerful coastal lights, before midnight; to my anxious eye it seemed to be too close under our lee, and fearful of becoming embayed near the political prison at Peniche, we altered course offshore to pass outside Berlenga, which before the days of radio beacons was the graveyard of many a ship. It turned into a wild night, and we shipped an occasional crest into the cockpit to soak the watchkeeper. Blondie was steering perfectly, but we had to keep a sharp look-out for shipping. We wondered how tiny *Dido* was getting on, and felt a little anxious for her; in fact, Bill and John

◀

6. While we were in Spanish waters our lunch on board always consisted of bread and cheese, wine, and grapes.

had wisely hove-to. Unknown to us then, our friends in *Valfreya* were also near by that night; it was their first experience of heavy weather, and talking about it afterwards John Cordiner said:

'There were breaking crests this high,' with an expressive gesture of his arm, 'each side of us, and astern a great pit as though a dozen navvies had been digging.'

We, having reached the big-ship lane, felt a little happier, and altering course to keep close inshore of it, we subsequently passed about 8 miles seaward of Ilha Berlenga. We were sorry not to stop at the island, but in such weather we thought it unwise, as its anchorage is rocky and restricted.

With the island astern the day improved, and by evening, when we were off Cabo Roca, Europe's most westerly mainland point, we were under full sail. But when we rounded the next headland and approached the mouth of the Tagus the wind sprang at us again, and as quickly as the work could be done we reduced sail to the close-reefed mainsail and second staysail. But now we were rapidly smoothing our water as we rushed along the coast at our maximum speed of 7 knots, heading for Cascais Bay, the summer anchorage under the northern shore, and hoped to arrive before nightfall. But we just missed doing that, and when the bay opened up we could not see what vessels were lying there because the battery of searchlights, which nightly is trained from the shore on to the anchorage to provide a pretty show for the holiday-makers, blinded us, and with our anemometer registering up to 40 knots this was no night to risk entanglement with yachts or fishing vessels. To reach comparative shelter we had to make one tack inshore, and as we put about we heard above the roar of the wind and the flapping of sails a splintering crack behind us, and looking aft in the searchlights' glare caught a glimpse of the upper two-thirds of the windvane taking off, broken clean across just above the balance arm. This was a grievous loss, but we had no time for mourning then, and I was worried about anchoring in so strong a wind, for *Wanderer* has no windlass or chain compresser, and it might be difficult to control the chain. However, Susan cleverly manoeuvred the ship so that with the reefed mainsail only just full she made little headway and slow leeway, and I had no difficulty except with the final few fathoms of chain, which had to be eased round the samson post link by link. Maybe I should have used a nylon rope instead of chain that night.

We did not sleep much for listening to the wind in the rigging, the spray rattling on deck, and the chain snatching in its fairlead, and for wondering how we could get a new and stronger vane made. But towards dawn the wind moderated, and on looking out at first light we saw ahead of us a gathering of yachts and fishing vessels, and beyond them the bright beaches and gaily coloured houses of Cascais, all dominated by a new skyscraper hotel. We had barely finished breakfast when a handsome woman in a club boat came alongside and introduced herself at Pat Potier; she said she had seen us approaching the previous evening, had recognized *Wanderer*, and had brought our mail. She took our dirty washing to be done, directed us to a vacant mooring close inshore, and invited us to lunch.

'Now, is there anything else you need?' she asked, as though she had not already shown us kindness enough.

So, of course, we told her about the broken windvane.

'Oh! that's quite easy,' she smiled. 'Tony, my husband, runs a shipyard, and if you let him know this evening exactly what you want he will have it made for you,' and she pushed off.

Pat Potier is English, her husband Portuguese; they live in a lovely, tree-shaded house with a swimming pool in the garden, they have three daughters, and they make it their business to look after visiting yachts. Within twenty-four hours a new vane had been built to my design, squatter and stronger than the original, but the ply of which it had been made was inferior and warped overnight. So Tony had a second one of thicker and better material made, and when I saw it I realized that I had not designed it of sufficient area; so I spent a day in the forepeak making for it what I call a bonnet—not a piece of headgear, but a close relation to a drabbler of squaresail days—which could be shipped on top of the standing vane and removed if necessary in heavy weather or in port, when, with the gear unlatched, the vane might flutter and rattle.

As our linen gets so disgustingly salt and dirty during a passage, we feel a little shy at handing it over to some nice stranger to get laundered. But in this instance we need not have worried; Pat got one of her maids to do it, and the report, which came from a Potier daughter, was: 'Nothing like so dirty as that from the last yacht, whose dishcloths were all stuck together.'

The Potiers were, as you can imagine, kindness itself, and so were the Ruggeronis (Portuguese Tony and American Anne) who have one of the houses overlooking the anchorage. Seated one evening in wicker chairs at the long refectory table there with the evening meal served by white-gloved parlourmaids, Susan and I felt that suddenly we had been transported back to early Victorian days. At dusk Tony got up and flicked a switch, so that the cliff, the rocks, and the beach immediately below the house glowed in warm light. I said that I preferred the scene without illumination, but he pointed out that this was necessary to prevent the place being used as a latrine by the locals, and, as he put it: 'No Portuguese will bare his buttocks in public.'

From mid-morning until sundown the tent-fringed beaches of Cascais were thronged with tan-seeking holiday-makers in gay trunks and bikinis; but at dawn they were deserted, the tents all closed, the sunshades furled. However, at sunrise there was life in plenty on the westernmost beach close to the great belching mouth of the sewer. There small boats under oars could be seen ferrying the night's catch ashore from the larger vessels lying off, each turning at the last moment to come in stern first. Chains of men carried the fish in shallow open boxes up the sand from which the tide had erased all traces of yesterday's scuffs and footprints, their busy forms reflected in its shining surface, and laid out the catch for auction. The fishwives made their bids, washed the long, glittering sabre fish in plastic buckets, arranged them with their other purchases artistically in large, flat baskets, lifted these on to their heads, and with stately tread made their barefoot way up to the cobbled streets to rouse the town with their strident cries.

Our friends gave us a great send-off and accompanied us several miles to sea when we set out for Madeira. The first twenty-four hours of the passage were boisterous, but the remaining three days were perfect. The wind was light then, and forward of the beam; there was no sea and no swell, and Blondie with new vane and bonnet attached steered all the way without any assistance from us, while we slept and ate and read. Clearly we should need to increase the size of our library for the longer passages.

At Funchal the pilot allotted us a somewhat exposed berth near the town jetty, where we rolled heavily and slept badly, but most of the better berths further in the harbour were occupied by local small craft, few of which appeared to be used, and much room is needed by the large passenger ships for the purpose of turning round before berthing at the mole. There were two single-handers, both Englishmen, preparing to make the Atlantic crossing: David Robertson in the 5-ton *Vagabond*, and David Guthrie with his corgi, Cider, in *Widgee*, one of the Laurent Giles Wanderer class, named after our *Wanderer* though not to the same design. David Robertson, lean, white-haired and softly spoken, had been knocking about in boats on and off for the past forty years; indeed, ever since he gave up his job as a London stockbroker when doctors told him he had only a short time to live. Between voyages he had grown grapes in the south of France and built houses in the Bahamas, and he claimed still to be the official harbourmaster at Stocking Island. He had bought *Vagabond* in Greece, and was now *en route* the hard way to visit his married son in Philadelphia. Also at Funchal was the 46-foot American ketch *Rena*. With her lovely sheer and graceful clipper bow she looked 'a million dollars', and must surely be one of the most beautiful vessels ever to come from John Alden's drawing board in Boston. Her owners, Commander and Mrs. Vancil, had built her entirely with their own hands, taking five years over the job, and were now returning to the U.S. after a European cruise.

As usual there was an area of calm south of Funchal when we left. We motored through this for an hour and then picked up not the expected moderate north or north-east wind, but half a gale from north-west, and with this on the quarter we ran fast to the south under reduced sail. The direction and strength of the wind, and the high north-west swell that accompanied it, prevented us from stopping at uninhabited Salvagem Grand, one of the group of small islands which lies half-way between Madeira and the Canaries. The islands have no lights, and we spent several hours of our first night hove-to, for although we had not yet run our distance by log, we had on another occasion in that area experienced a $1\frac{1}{4}$-knot south-setting current, and we had no wish to make contact with the islands in the dark. In daylight we sighted them, passed to the westward, and a day later came to the busy commercial and fishing port of La Luz, the port for Las Palmas on Gran Canaria.

This is a favourite jumping-off place for west-bound yachts, and here among other Atlantic candidates we found *Northern Light* (the girls' white uniforms were still miraculously white), *Dido* (very interested in *Northern Light*), and Humphrey Barton with a two-girl crew in *Rose Rambler*, which was shortly to start on her fifth crossing.

The old Club Nautico was being pulled down in clouds of dust along with other buildings; large apartment blocks were going up, a new club had been built at the exposed, seaward end of the port. A trickle of fresh water was available only every other day, and parties from the yachts queued for it. Smuts from the many streamers rained upon us, begriming decks and rigging, and after the simple operation of taking in the ensign at sundown one needed a wash; the water, the walls, and the landing steps were thickly coated with oil, and if La Luz is not the dirtiest harbour in the world it must be so nearly so as to make little difference. But, of course, we had no right to complain, for nobody had asked us to go there, and at least the traffic-torn, littered town did provide all manner of British and American food and drink at very low prices, for it is a free port.

With some work to attend to, we had to remain for two weeks. In an attempt to improve our lot we moved to the outside anchorage off the club, but that was not a success, for although the water was clean when we went there, and we were able to bathe and clean the ship, the following day a considerable swell rolled in, and someone discharged quantities of thick oil in which *Wanderer* literally wallowed; we even got some of this on the deck when two swimmers, their bodies glistening with it, climbed aboard uninvited over the stern. The swell and the oil made landing at the steel ladders of the club pier hazardous, and we returned to the inner harbour even filthier than we had been before. At about this time *Dido*'s crew put her on the beach so that they might scrub and antifoul her bottom. This was done, but as the tide started to rise the oil came in and rose with it, so that *Dido*'s entire freshly painted bottom became coated with oil. I wondered, and so no doubt did Bill and John, whether oil possesses any antifouling properties.

Susan and I hoped that Santa Cruz, on the neighbouring island of Tenerife, might provide cleaner and less disturbed conditions in which to make our final preparations for the ocean passage which lay ahead, and decided to go there. Before we had finished breakfast on the day set for our departure, Cherry, the eldest of the Griffin daughters, from *Northern Light*, came over and insisted on cleaning the oil off *Wanderer*'s sides; she was soon followed by June (the next in order of age) who collected our cans and undertook the tiresome job of getting them filled with fresh water. Such spontaneous kindness from such young people touched us; but alas! Cherry's labours were in vain, for before we could get away the steep wash from the fast pilot launches had made our sides just as oily as before.

After an almost completely calm fortnight there was a fresh north-east wind blowing the evening we left, but at sea, as so often happens near high islands, it died, and we motored in confused water to the north end of the island. There a new wind from the west pounced on us with near gale strength, and we, well reefed and hard on the wind, and only just able to lay the course, had such a wet and uncomfortable time that after an hour or so we turned back for La Luz, but only to run into the same calm patch that we had so recently left. Clearly nothing was to be gained by motoring back to the oily harbour, so once again we turned, hardened our hearts, and plunged wetly on our way. Of course, we got becalmed again next morning when we came into the lee of Tenerife, for that really is a high island even if you exclude its 12,000-foot peak. As we approached Santa Cruz under power we were horrified to see eight big tankers at the anchorage where they discharge their cargo, and to come into a slick of oil which extended at least five miles from the land.

Our motor had developed further trouble in that the gear lever was now jammed in the ahead position, from which we could not budge it, and as the only way of stopping was to stop the motor, manoeuvring under power was clearly out of the question; so we stopped the motor outside and sailed with squally puffs of hot wind in to a berth where we lay with anchors out ahead and a stern line to a buoy in a very crowded corner. Though there was plenty of oil about, the place was not quite so dirty as La Luz, but the wash from local craft made work aloft so difficult that when we left several rigging jobs, including the fitting of chafing gear to the crosstree ends, had not been done. It certainly is unfortunate that the Canary Islands, conveniently situated as they are, and with cheap stores of every kind readily available, do not provide a single clean anchorage where a small yacht can attend to her own simple needs in complete security. Santa Cruz de la Palma, which we had visited in 1952, is, we are told, still clean and unspoilt, but it is open to winds from south and might then become untenable.

▶

7. At sunrise the night's catch is brought ashore on the western beach at Cascais, from which the tide has erased all traces of yesterday's footprints, so that the busy figures are reflected in its shining surface.

3

IN THE NORTH-EAST TRADE WIND

Lat. 18°59′N., long. 32°30′W.
30 October

A warm wind blows from aft to forward through the cabin, fluttering the paper in the typewriter and keeping the temperature down to 80°F.; a rectangle of brilliant sunlight, entering through the wide-open companionway, slashes from side to side across the galley bench and chart table as the ship rolls. From forward comes the steady roar of a 5-knot bow-wave, and from aft the hiss of breaking crests as the seas overtake us; there is a rumbling and gurgling of water in the tanks. Susan has just squeezed our daily oranges, and now, her bare feet planted wide apart on the scrubbed galley floor, the moving sunlight striking highlights in her auburn hair each time it swings across, is humming to herself as she peels the potatoes, which I hope she is going to fry, for lunch.

Wanderer is running under her white twin sails with Blondie steering; she is in the heart of the north-east trade wind and in a part of the ocean which she knows well, for at noon today she will be very near the position she had occupied on 23 October 1952 (when making her first trip to the West Indies), and 15 May 1955 (when on passage from Ascension Island to

◀

8. *Top:* Over a blue and easy sea in proper trade-wind weather the ship averages 100 miles a day as she makes her Atlantic crossing. All of the steering was done by the vane gear, which was designed by Blondie Hasler. *Bottom:* The offset plywood vane is connected to the trim-tab on the rudder by means of a toothed wheel and latch (for adjustment) and a link.

the Azores). These positions, marked by crosses on the well-used and rather grubby North Atlantic chart, almost coincide. Another cross some 200 miles to the south shows where she was on 22 October 1959 when on passage from the Cape Verde Islands to the Demerara River. I wonder what she thinks about it all as she rolls along.

To make this passage is the dream of many folk less fortunate than ourselves, and it is usually regarded by small-boat people as being the easiest and most enjoyable of all the trade wind passages of the world. This opinion is confirmed by the October and November pilot charts—those remarkable documents which, by means of coloured symbols, tell the strength and direction of the winds and currents which over a period of many years have been experienced by seamen in each five-degree square—for they show that about 90 per cent of all winds encountered in the area have an easterly component and an average strength of force 4, a moderate breeze, and that gales are rare. The charts suggest that one might expect to pick up a fair wind among or shortly after leaving the Canary Islands; if one uses this to make latitude 25°N. in about 25°W. longitude, one should then be well within the trade wind boundary and able with advantage to head in a more westerly direction towards one's destination. But this October the weather has been unusual in that the trade wind went out of business in the eastern part of the ocean; we have therefore had some difficulty in reaching our present position (see chart on pages 4 and 5); indeed, although we have now been at sea for nearly a fortnight, we have made good only 1,000 miles.

With the customary feelings of excitement mixed with apprehension, we left Santa Cruz in the morning on 17 October, bound towards Barbados 2,700 miles away. Outside the harbour we found a moderate headwind, and all that day we turned to windward to get through the wide channel which separates Gran Canaria and Tenerife. It was a disheartening beginning to a long passage, but worse was to follow, for after we had cleared the islands the wind dropped to a light air, and often, mostly at night, there were long periods of calm. Under our maximum sail area of 600 square feet, we crept slowly and silently along by day on the starboard tack, for clearly it was necessary to make southing rather than westing now if we were ever going to find the trade wind, and sometimes we motored for an hour or two; but our fuel supply is small, and we wished to conserve some of it for battery-charging during the voyage. However, apart from lack of wind the weather was lovely: cool, crisp, and dry, and the pale sky was free of cloud. Each evening we sat together in the cockpit, discussing the small happenings of the day while we sipped our drinks and watched the naked sun grow distorted, sometimes becoming pear-shaped, sometimes flat like a flying saucer, just before he plunged below the horizon. Twice we saw the green flash as the sun went down, and on one occasion it was repeated in quick succession due to the swell lifting us up at the crucial moment. Each night we hung the riding light in the rigging and both slept soundly, for these were the first silent nights we had enjoyed for a month. Nevertheless our slow progress was disturbing, for one eats and drinks just as much whether headway is being made or not, and in so small a vessel one cannot carry an unlimited supply of food and water. We called to mind other voyagers who had experienced unfavourable weather on this passage, and remembered that the late Admiral Goldsmith in *Diotima* took 44 days, having 7 days of calm and 4 of headwind, and that more recently Tom and Janet Steele in *Adios* were becalmed for 20 days. We were more fortunate, for with us the quiet conditions lasted for only 4 days. During the second day the cloud on Tenerife dissolved, and we saw its peak clearly when 75 miles away; from such a distance this is a rare sight except during the months of January and February. On the third day out, when we made a run of only 27 miles, we could still see Hierro, the south-westernmost of the islands.

However, we had plenty of jobs to keep us busy. With paraffin and rags we cleaned as much of the oil as we could reach off the topsides, and we washed away the dust and sand and soot; and what a pleasure it was when drawing a bucket of water or flushing the heads to find the sea absolutely clean and clear. There were letters and one hundred Christmas cards to be written and addressed, films to develop, fruit to sort and wrap, and some brightwork to varnish.

After the fourth night of calm a breeze made from north-east, and for the first time we were then able to ease sheets, set one of the twin sails, and make good the desired course. Could this, we asked each other, be the trade wind at last? Fearful that it might hear us and die, we spoke in whispers and moved on tiptoe. In fact, it lasted for only three days, during which we achieved daily runs in excess of 100 miles, and felt we were making reasonable progress.

But when I looked out at dawn of the fourth day I saw a big, black cloud, trailing a slanting skirt of rain, advancing upon us from the east. At sea under sail, and particularly in the tropics, such things are a nuisance, always an anxiety, and occasionally a danger, for they interfere with the strength and direction of the wind; but although Susan and I have kept our eyes on many hundreds of them in our time, we still cannot judge whether the wind will back or veer, freshen or die away. If we had reduced sail each time a rain cloud approached, we would have put ourselves to a lot of unnecessary trouble and spoilt many a day's run, for the majority have no vice in them. But occasionally such a cloud, although it looks no different from the others, may bring not only rain but a squall of gale-force wind. When that happens it usually comes suddenly, perhaps at the first onset of rain, and hoping that it will be of short duration, we may decide to hang on to full sail; the hard-pressed ship becomes wild on the helm as she rushes through the grey, spume-covered sea with a great bow-wave building up each side; the watchkeeper feels he has to stand by the vane gear in case it may need help, turning from time to time with eyes screwed up against the horizontal rain, to peer to windward, hoping to see a lightening of the gloom. When this occurs 'Stars to windward' is the cry, and we can both relax. But if the squall is long sustained, the watchkeeper's nerve may fail him; he shouts for his companion to come to the helm, and with yellow oilskins flapping round him (if he has managed to put them on in time) makes his way forward to reef or hand the sails, wishing as he struggles with them that he had done this earlier. It is the squall that strikes by night which is likely to be most dangerous for us, because we are probably both in our bunks then, sleeping, and the first we know about it is a rattle of rain on deck, a whining of wind in the rigging, and the urgent noise of rapid progress. But we are not in the habit of carrying a press of sail, and it is a matter of only a moment before one or other of us is looking out to see if a reduction of sail is called for. When at last the rain stops and the black cloud draws ahead, it probably takes all the wind along with it, leaving the sullenly slatting sails to steam in the greenhouse atmosphere, and the compass binnacle fogged so that one feels curiously lost as to direction. However, on this particular morning the cloud brought little extra wind, so we closed the hatches and ports to keep the rain out, thus making nonsense of the ventilation system, and in a steamy fug boiled our breakfast eggs, cut the mildewed crust off a loaf and made the toast. By the time we had finished so had the wind, so we took the opportunity to hand the mainsail and examine it for chafe, and Susan sewed on a patch where it had been rubbing against the unprotected upper crosstrees.

For this voyage we had replaced the old heavy solid wooden boom with a light one of alloy, and this was the first time we had had occasion to lower the mainsail while rolling about out in the open sea; we found this light spar much easier and safer to deal with, also it is quieter in a calm, for the foot of the sail is held in a groove instead of by slides on a track. Unfortunately the new and expensive enclosed-type roller reefing gear with which it is fitted is not a success, for it has become stiff and hard to turn in spite of plenty of lubrication; so we shall have to dismantle it to see what is wrong, but not out here with this violent motion. I regret now having parted with the old Appledore gear, which although clumsy never failed us in fourteen years of hard use.

After that rain the trade wind did not blow steadily again for three days, but now at last we do appear to be in the heart of it and sailing fast. We are running under the twin sails, not because Blondie needs any assistance in steering, but so as to save the mainsail from chafe and preserve it for sterner things to come, the wind being dead aft. When we came to set the second of the twin sails we discovered that one of the jobs I failed to get done at Santa Cruz was to reeve its halyard; so we have had to use the genoa masthead halyard instead, but this seems to make no difference. The twin sails are silent and cannot chafe on anything, but under them alone the ship does roll heavily, so we have set the trysail as well, an ancient heavy flax sail of only 75 square feet, and sheeted it flat amidships, its single-part sheets leading through blocks near the ends of the mainsheet horse, then forward to the headsail sheet winches. This has made life not exactly comfortable, but certainly less uncomfortable than it was, for it has taken the jerk out of the roll and lengthened the period a little. In the days before we had Blondie it was not possible to have the trysail set as well as the twin sails unless we were prepared to take over the steering, for it interfered with their self-steering properties. But Blondie takes not the slightest notice of the little brown steadying sail as it gybes silently and repeatedly, and continues to hold the ship on or near her downwind course.

This morning before I settled in with my typewriter I spent some time on deck, leaning over the guardrails up forward and watching the stem slice purposefully through the ocean. As the sun was shining from a clear sky, the sea was real deep-sea blue, and looking straight down into it I could see it was intensely clear and that it had a suggestion of mauve in its colouring. Against it the bow-waves each side—steady cascades of tumbling water, sometimes rising almost to deck-level, sometimes dropping a long way down the copper sheathing—were startlingly white; abreast the shrouds these waves subsided to form lacy patterns flowing quickly to mingle in the wake and climb the face of the next overtaking sea. At the stern Blondie's varnished vane, a striking contrast to the blue of sea and sky, stood tall and lean facing aft, yet moving just a little one way or the other as the ship yawed, so as to move the link gear and the trim tab to bring her firmly back on course, the tiller moving to and fro as though some invisible hand controlled it. Seventy feet astern, at the end of its thin white line, the spinning log rotator was sometimes just visible high up on a crest or down in a hollow; but beyond that we left no mark on the wrinkled face of the indifferent ocean to show that we had passed that way. Sea and sky may well have looked just as they do today a million years ago.

Lat. 14°25′N., long. 50°30′W.
8 November

The sun burns down harshly from a thinly veiled sky, making the deck too hot for bare feet, and the humidity is so great that our bodies cannot refrigerate in the normal manner; drops of salt sweat trickle into our eyes. There is a breeze, a very light one on the quarter, and a swell from the same direction, and as this runs under and lifts the ship the mainsail is thrown hard aback, but only to refill a few seconds later. Sometimes the noise of this is prolonged a little like a roll of thunder, but more often it is sudden and startling like the crack of a whip. This happens at from ten- to twenty-second intervals, and every slat of the terylene sail shakes the mast and through that the whole structure of the vessel. One of the twins set the opposite side is also thrown aback by the swell, but as I have already said it is light and small and can touch nothing, so it makes very little noise and does not chafe itself. Unfortunately the wind is too far out on the quarter to permit the other twin to be set. We make good a speed of only about 2 knots.

These conditions have prevailed for the past twenty-four hours, preventing sleep and causing more wear and tear on gear and nerves than a whole gale. Even gentle-natured Susan is a bit irritable, and wonders why the hell we don't have a bigger boat with more power and fuel, so at least we could drown the din of flogging sails and make some worthwhile progress. However, we did have our money's worth last week, running for seven days under the twins and trysail, and never having to touch a sheet, brace, or guy in all that time. That really was something for nothing, and then we could spend all night in our bunks if we wanted to, though each of us usually looked out several times to see that the riding light, hung on the boom gallows, was burning brightly, and to scan the horizon for the lights of other ships.

But an occasional look-out such as this is, of course, of very little use, for naval and commercial ships move fast, and if we and one of these happen to be approaching one another end on, ten-minute intervals between one look-out and the next are quite long enough. We both consider that since the advent of radar, by means of which a ship can see other ships around her as points of light on a darkened screen, the chance of being run down by a large vessel is the greatest of all hazards to which small yachts are exposed, for most merchant ships now do not keep a proper look-out at sea, and for steering rely not on a human who might occasionally look out through the wheel-house windows, but on an automatic pilot. No doubt the officer of the watch will look from time to time at his radar screen, but on this the small wooden yacht does not show up at all well, and in rough weather may not be sufficiently visible there to catch his eye among the wave clutter. Besides, he is not expecting to meet tiny vessels. A radar reflector aboard the yacht will help to show her more clearly on the screen, but is no guarantee of her safety. A large vessel's white range lights are high and powerful, and therefore may be seen from a considerable distance; but a yacht cannot exhibit such powerful lights, and the red and green sidelights, which are laid down by international law for her use when under sail, may perhaps not be visible for more than a mile, and because of their low situation may often be hidden by intervening seas. Maybe this does not matter a great deal, as nobody is likely to be looking for them anyway,

▶

9. *Top:* I look out from the hatchway at night to see if the riding light hung on the boom gallows is burning brightly, and to scan the horizon for the lights of other ships. On this occasion the mainsail is stowed and coated and the ship is running under twin sails, but to steady her the trysail is also set and sheeted flat amidships; its clew can just be seen. *Bottom:* By night flying-fish come aboard to flap their short life out in the scuppers; this one, ten inches long, was the largest we ever found on deck in the morning.

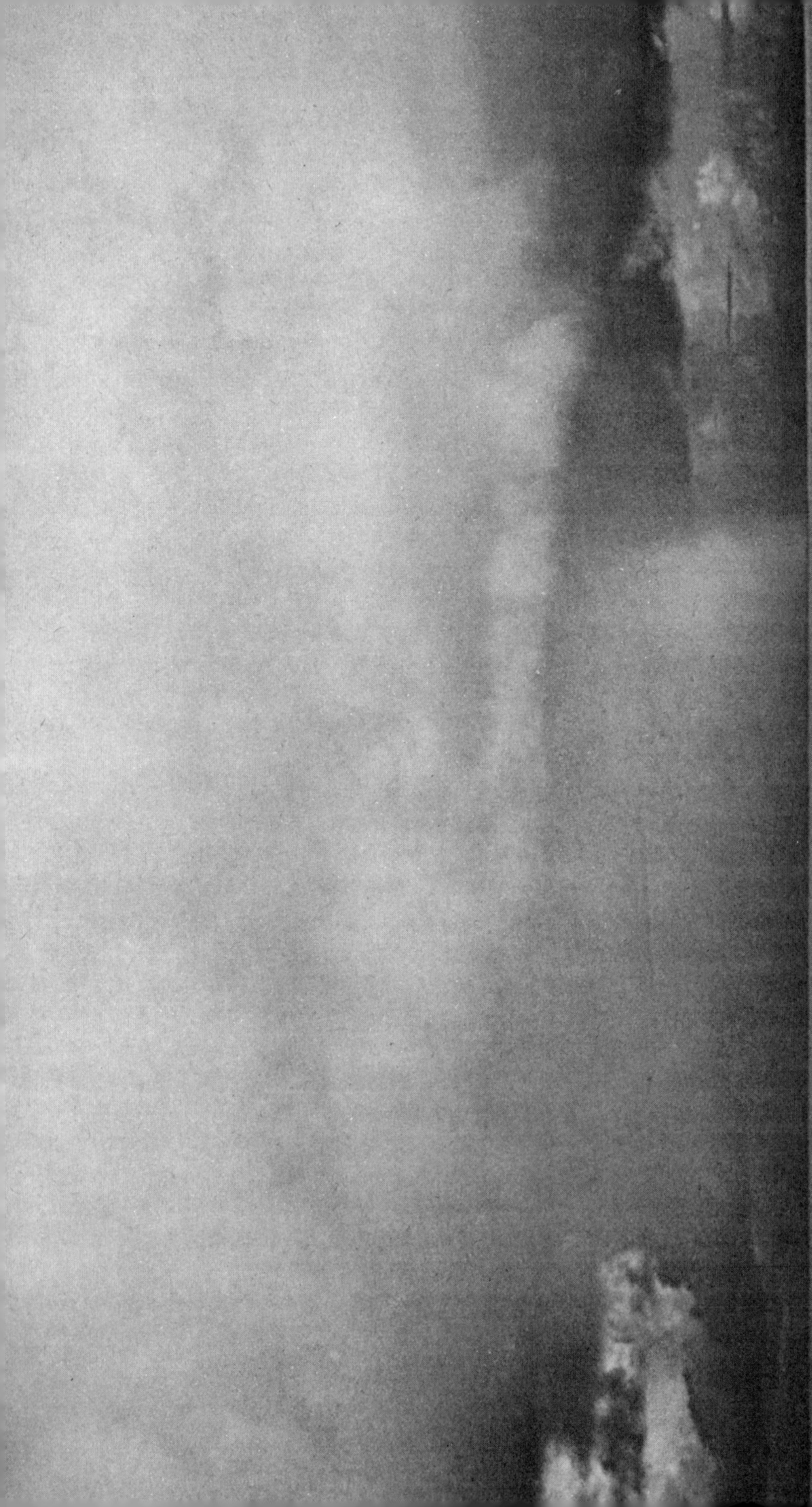

but we feel happier with a single white light which can more easily be seen if anyone *is* looking.

In view of all this you may, if you are not a sailing man yourself, well ask how we can feel sufficiently at ease both to sleep at the same time. Fortunately for ocean-going yachts and their people, merchant ships do tend to keep more or less to certain lanes, and these are shown on the appropriate charts. So when we are on or near a lane we keep our ten-minute look-out. This would apply, for example, on the great circle course from New York or the North-east Providence Channel to the English Channel, and we would be punctilious about it, never relaxing the look-out by day or by night, for the risk of being run down appears to be almost as great in full daylight as it is on the darkest night. But the trade wind route across the Atlantic is not used by commercial shipping, and only a few recognized lanes cut across it. There is also this to be said about keeping a look-out: for the first night or two a look-out may seem essential, but after you have kept a proper look-out over that period and have not seen a thing you begin to realize the size and emptiness of the ocean, and unless the crew is large you are beginning to feel tired; then the desire for sleep overcomes the fear of collision. Perhaps the greatest risk today on the Atlantic trade wind crossing is the chance of collision with some overtaking or overtaken yacht, she, like ourselves, with a white light hung up and all her company fast asleep down below, for many now make the crossing each year in the months of October and November, and most have some form of automatic steering device.

One of the sad things about using a vane steering gear and keeping no permanent look-out is that one misses much of the beauty and peace of the ocean night. No longer do we look entranced at the phosphorescent wake streaming out astern between glances at the compass by which we are steering; no longer do we lie on our back on a cockpit seat admiring the

◀

10. A black cloud trailing a slanting skirt of rain advanced upon us from the east. In the tropics such things are always an anxiety and occasionally a danger.

beauty of the star-filled heavens, identifying old star friends—perhaps useful for navigation—and discovering new ones; no longer do we watch the full moon polish a silver path astern and etch the shapes of sails and rigging black across the slanting deck, or see her plunge into the sea ahead as the sun rises astern. We hog it in our frowsty bunks. But then what a pleasure it is in the morning to wake wide-eyed and full of energy, instead of being bleary and numb. And, of course, because we do not have to spend long hours at night steering, the occasional visit to the deck during the dark hours now holds a special attraction, and sometimes when I have woken and made my way to the hatch I have found Susan already sitting in the cockpit. Had some sudden or unusual noise woken us? Some premonition of danger—a floating log, perhaps, or another vessel? I think not; the meeting was just by chance or because we had both had our fill of sleep.

Susan puts her firm, warm hand on mine and says: 'No ships, no squalls, and what a heavenly night. I wonder where the others from La Luz have got to. Must all be out here somewhere', gesturing vaguely around. '*Northern Light*, *Dido*, *Rose Rambler*, and the rest. Are they, too, enjoying it, do you think?'

After a bit conversation lapses; we yawn, have one more look round, then creep back into our bunks.

So you see we have not been keeping a proper look-out, and there may well have been more ships passing while we slept than ever we imagined; but apart from one tanker hull down when we were four days out from Tenerife, we have seen nothing, and this appears to be the experience of most other yachts on this particular route, even of those that do keep a look-out. But we shall have to mind our step when we cruise in the more highly populated waters off the American coast.

So far only a few flying-fish have come aboard by night to flap their short lives out in the scuppers, but never enough of them at one time to make a meal, and we have seen only one school of porpoises. Of birds we have seen only storm petrels and a tropic (or bosun) bird, which visited us on two successive mornings. I fear our bright riding light tends to confuse the petrels, for we have had two come aboard, one in the cockpit and the other down in the cabin, where it made an astonishing mess for one so small in such a short time. Both seemed to be dazed, and Susan had no difficulty in catching them and getting them airborne to leeward.

It was an uneventful period, but we had the satisfaction of making good progress and the interest of the various displays which nature staged. Only sometimes did the sky look as one supposes it ought to look in trade wind areas, that is, bright blue with small, puffy cumulus clouds chasing one another across it. More often there has been much torn cirrus; there have been solar and lunar halos, and sometimes complete overcast with here and there huge patches of almost black sky with dirty-white clouds scurrying along beneath them. Such things looked threatening, and so did many of the flaming sunrises and sunsets, but for the whole of that week none of these signs of wrath made the slightest difference to the wind, which mostly was fresh and from a little north of east and with occasional strong squalls. On four successive nights we saw in the south-east a little before dawn a comet with a magnificent tail ten degrees in length as measured by sextant; it gave the impression of plunging earthward through the night sky, though it had no discernible movement. The *Nautical Almanac* made no mention of this lovely and remarkable thing, and the B.B.C. World Service, which we were able to receive at certain times of day on the 31-metre band, was so packed with international gloom and doom that it had no time to mention it.

Our pleasant progress could not be expected to continue indefinitely, and at dawn on the eighth day of running under twins and trysail the whole sky became uniform blue-black as though it was burdened with ink, and for many hours there was a heavy downpour of rain. This, of course, killed the wind and left us slamming helplessly in the left-over sea. That was two days ago, and since then we have had very little wind.

By yesterday we had been at sea for three weeks, and the distances made good during those three weeks were 558, 661, and 880 miles—nothing very remarkable. But we are now well on to the western sheet of the North Atlantic chart, with Barbados lying only 530 miles ahead. Cheered by last week's good progress, we worked out our estimated time of arrival, and decided on Friday evening so that we could have a night at anchor and then collect our mail on Saturday before the bank closed. But now with so little wind to push us along we do begin to wonder. It is a curious fact that although so many of us dream of making long voyages in little ships, no sooner have we got properly started than our every thought and effort is directed to the moment of arrival and the quiet anchorage we hope to find.

At Barbados
15 November

We have just been over the side to remove with scraper and brush some of the many goose barnacles, which have adhered to and grown large upon our antifouled copper sheathing during the Atlantic crossing; here in Carlisle Bay, where the water over the sandy bottom is an exquisite pale green and warm enough to be a caress, such an occupation is a real pleasure. Indeed, little excuse is needed for a bathe, and many times a day we slip over the side to swim and cool off, admiring as we do so the pleasing lines of the trim and able little ship which brought us here. Inshore of us lies the inevitable fleet of rarely used speed-boats and other small craft which in these days of mass boat production choke so many good anchorages; beyond them the squat, gaily painted pier of the friendly Aquatic Club thrusts out into the bay.

I suppose that a period of several weeks in the clean and lonely ocean, away from sight or sound of other human beings, is not the best preparation for an arrival at a great many places, including present-day Barbados. So we were upset to find this gay and once lovely bay, which provides the best anchorage and probably the pleasantest and safest bathing in the island, now dominated by an oil refinery, its dull roar almost drowning the merry cries of the bathers and the bell-like notes of the tree frogs, and by a large erection which we are told is to be a hotel.

The final stage of our passage was made at reasonable speed after all, although there was a lot of sail drill due to the wind becoming unsteady in strength and direction, and always we were bothered by the swell which came from some other direction than the wind. We covered the last 500 miles at just over 100 miles a day, but those final days did not hold for us the pleasure of the earlier ones, for we were now tiring of the ceaseless motion, against which it was at all times necessary to hang on tightly or wedge oneself securely; the more interesting and palatable items of food had been consumed, and the best books in our library had all been read; in fact, we were almost bored. During the night of our twenty-sixth day at sea we made our landfall on Ragged Point light—a difficult one to time, as it flashes only once in every two minutes—at the eastern tip of the island. Just as on other occasions I, as navigator, experienced a sense of satisfaction coupled with some astonishment that my observations of the very distant sun from an unsteady platform and the use of some simple tables (I still use the old but excellent *Astronomical Navigation Tables*, which unfortunately for yachtsmen are no longer published) enable a small island to be found with certainty after an ocean crossing.

On this passage, as on others where the weather is mostly fine and one can be fairly certain of getting observations of the sun when needed, my navigational routine was simple indeed. Each morning, usually two hours or so before noon, I took a sight, worked it out, and drew the resulting position line on a Baker's plotting diagram, the ocean chart being on too small a scale to be used accurately for the purpose. At local noon I observed the sun's meridian passage to obtain our latitude. Bringing the morning position line forward along the course made good to the extent of the distance run since the morning sight was taken, the point where it crossed the noon latitude was our noon position. On the rare occasions when the sun was obscured by cloud at noon I took the sight as near noon as possible and worked it out to obtain an ordinary position line.

As the patent log was towed all the time to show the distance sailed through the water it was easy to see whether there had been any current since the previous day's fix, and if so how much and in what direction it had been setting. On this trip the current averaged about 10 miles a day in a westerly direction. Of course, a fix got by taking observations of the stars is a little more accurate because the sights are taken within a few moments of one another and no allowance has to be made for the distance sailed between them; but such sights are more difficult to take, especially in the tropics, where twilight is short, and often the sails get in the way; so I do not normally bother with them unless I have failed to get sun sights when about to make a landfall.

We arrived three days ago, not as we had originally hoped on Friday, but first thing on Saturday, and might still have collected our mail before the bank closed had not Barbados officialdom increased in volume in keeping with its fine new big-ship port, and all the forenoon was occupied getting entered.

4

CHARTER FLEET WATERS

In the late 1940s Commander Vernon Nicholson, with his wife Emmie and sons Rodney and Desmond, set out from England in the schooner *Mollihawk* to make the classic North Atlantic circuit—to the West Indies by the trade wind route and home via Bermuda—but they never completed that trip. On the south coast of Antigua they came almost casually to landlocked English Harbour, where the quays and buildings of an eighteenth-century British naval dockyard lay deserted and partly in ruins; they did some work on the ship and grew so to like the place that they stayed on there, and it has been *Mollihawk*'s home port ever since. Now and then a few of the Americans who were vacationing on the island found their way to the dockyard, and some of them asked to be taken for a sail in the handsome old black schooner with the clipper bow and raking varnished masts, which looked so perfect and appropriate in that historic setting. Vernon was quite willing, and two of his earlier paying guests were Mr. and Mrs. Macey, a name famous in America where big chain stores are concerned. (The last time I saw them they were driving about the harbour in an amphibious car.)

Thus began the yacht chartering business in those waters, and soon a second vessel was acquired to cope with the increasing demand. Vernon and Emmie established themselves on the upper floor of the pay office—one of the few dockyard buildings that still had a roof on it—to attend to inquiries and organization, and by radio telephone kept in touch with their sons who were skippering the two yachts. There are along the chain of Windward and Leeward Islands only a few harbours

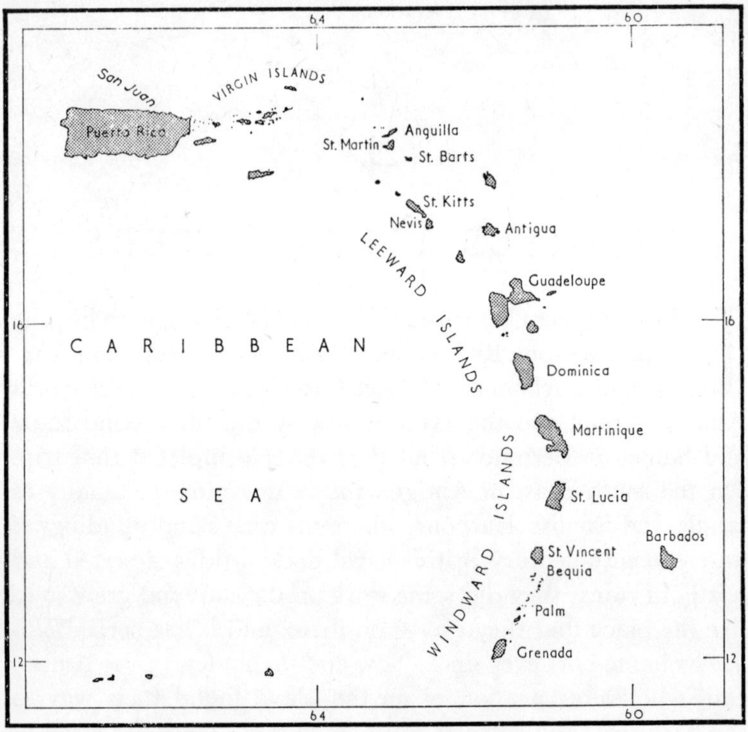

WEST INDIES

which provide good shelter in hurricanes; of these English Harbour is probably the best (this was the chief reason for its selection as a naval base) and here in 1950 *Mollihawk* safely rode out the two hurricanes which did considerable damage to the old buildings.

Rapidly word of the Irish charm of the Nicholsons, the efficient and seamanlike manner in which their yachts were conducted, and the delights of cruising among those islands, spread in the United States, and each winter more and more Americans wanted to charter. So Vernon added to his fleet, not by buying

▶

11. *Top:* With adze and hand-saw, for they have no power tools, men of Bequia build a 70-foot schooner on the beach at Friendship. *Bottom:* The schooner *Adonis* unloads a Land-Rover at the little jetty in Admiralty Bay.

more yachts, but by persuading owners of yachts to take paying guests, he acting as agent on a commission basis. I do not think he can ever have had much difficulty in finding a supply of willing owners, for each year yachts cross from Europe or come down from the States, and often their owners are young and impecunious and are only too happy to earn some tax-free money in this way. They imagine that a few weeks' work (if, they think, one can call it work) taking pleasant guests up and down the island chain in almost perfect weather will enable them to live aboard and enjoy their yachts undisturbed for the rest of the year. They soon discover, of course, that there is more to it than this, and that to be attractive to would-be charterers a yacht must be well found and well run, and that much of the charter fees have to be spent on maintenance, improvements, and crews' wages. Also a good deal of tact and a sense of humour is required so that one can happily accept the role of cook, steward, and barman as well as that of skipper.

From his simple start with *Mollihawk* Vernon Nicholson has steadily increased his business, and today has more than forty yachts for charter under his control, while other agents have started up elsewhere. Some of these yachts are or have been run by people we had met during our voyages, names now famous in the cruising world. Edward Allcard, for example, the bearded English single-hander, rarely lacked for guests, for his writings describing his desperate fights for survival in the Atlantic and his glamorous Azorean stowaway had not passed unnoticed in America. He chartered for several years and then sailed on alone to round Cape Horn. But generally the yachts which get most bookings are those run by married couples, and of these two of the most popular have been *Fjording* and *Outward Bound*. *Fjording* was originally a steel ferry boat and was converted to

◀

12. *Wanderer* sails past the old dockyard at English Harbour, where some of the fleet of charter yachts are lying. The small building immediately behind her is the galley, and near it stand two of the capstans which were used for careening ships. In the background at the left is the Admiral's house, now a museum, and on the right some of the great stone pillars which are all that remain of the boathouse. I took this photograph from near Clarence House, the point from which we watched (and unwittingly took part in) a performance of *son et lumière*.

a comfortable motor/sailer by her owners, the Swedish couple Sten and Brita Holmdahl. They made a two-year circumnavigation of the world in their first boat, the ketch *Viking*, at the same time as Susan and I were making our first voyage. I recently asked Brita if she did not find some of the charterers a little difficult to live with and to satisfy, and her answer revealed one of the secrets of *Fjording*'s success.

'Eric,' she said in her clipped but perfect English, 'they are *all* nice people.'

The popularity of the Holmdahls is probably equalled by that of John and Mary Caldwell. Many years ago we met them in the Pacific, where they were making a leisurely voyage and rearing a family. On arrival in Australia (she is an Australian, he American) they built with their own hands the ketch *Outward Bound*, sailed her by way of the Red Sea to the West Indies, and there chartered with great success. But John and Mary now live ashore on Palm Island, one of the Grenadines, which they are developing as a beach club, and, as one might expect of such practical and energetic people, have done tremendous works there, such as making an air-strip and a water-catchment; they have completed a beach bar, several cabanas and a few houses, and at present employ a labour force of one hundred. They are indeed remarkable people, and let no opportunities slip no matter how much work may be involved. As an example of this I quote from a letter we recently had from John:

> Do you remember *Windwife*? John Lucas was sailing her single-handed from Grenada to Antigua when he fell overboard to the eastward of Palm Island, and the yacht struck on our south-east point. John swam ashore safely and we salvaged everything including the hull. We loosened the keel-bolts, slipped the iron ballast keel, and using a chain hoist dragged the sunken hull over the reef and lagoon to the beach. I bought the wreck and we are now repairing her to make a launch for transporting our men.

Some people prefer not to employ an agent but to organize their own charters, and many of these, like our friends Ross and Doreen Norgrove from New Zealand in their big schooner *White Squall*, sail out of St. Thomas in the American Virgin Islands, a place which has always been popular among free-lances, and in its early days had some strange characters; the rum flowed pretty freely then, and nudist parties were not uncommon.

All kinds of people charter, and with varying degrees of success. Retired officers from the services; a night-club entertainer, whose wife (caterer and cook) was on one occasion given a tip of $300 by an appreciative guest; young men who, apart from a boat, seem to possess little but good looks and a guitar; a few are well-to-do owners who send their yachts with crews to the West Indies to charter when they do not need them themselves. In this community feuds are not uncommon, and one section may not be on speaking terms with another. But we, in the fortunate position of strangers with no axe to grind, had the entrée to both camps, and most of the charter people we met seemed pleased to see us and were hospitable, though once or twice we did gain the impression that we had been invited aboard only to provide entertainment for the guests.

Barbados, where we spent a week buying provisions and other things we needed, and rolling heavily at times when the wind hauled round a little too far to the south, is an outrider of the West Indies, and therefore is rarely visited by charter yachts; but we soon came into their field of operations, and some we met so often that we got to know which side the generating engine's exhaust was placed, and when possible anchored away from it. A generating plant is an important item of a charter yacht's equipment, for she needs a refrigerator and a deep freeze so that she can carry adequate supplies of fine meat—this is often cooked on a charcoal fire on deck—and other fresh provisions, and frequently such equipment calls for several hours of battery charging each day.

From Barbados we made a pleasant 100-mile downwind trip overnight to the island of Bequia, and in the morning worked our way into the peaceful anchorage in well-sheltered Admiralty Bay. Seven years had passed since our last visit, and we found the place little changed, the small island community going unhurried about its simple business. The people were still polite and friendly, and that was something we found lacking in other islands which were British at that time. The ferry boats *Whistler* and *Bequia Transport* made their daily trips to neighbouring St. Vincent, and the schooners *Adonis* and *Turtle Dove* came and went about their inter-island affairs. The same old woman baked bread for us in her 44-gallon kerosene drum oven, and each morning sternly drove her pig down to the sea for a bathe. With adze and hand-saw, for they still have no power tools, some of the same men were building a 70-foot schooner under the trees on the beach over at Friendship. The only noticeable difference was that there were now many more visiting yachts, for Bequia is one of the islands in the gently curving chain linking Antigua in the north with Grenada in the south, and this is the cruising ground of the charter fleets. It was still early in the season, and several yachts run by married couples were enjoying a sort of honeymoon cruise before work started. The presence of these immaculate craft emphasized *Wanderer*'s need of a refit; this we planned to do in English Harbour, and we soon headed that way.

With few exceptions the islands which lie between Bequia and Antigua are high—some with 4,000-feet mountains—and to sail through their lee is often difficult; depending on the strength of the trade wind and on how much north or south it happens to have in it, there may be a big area of headwind, light airs, or calm, and usually at some stage there is a short jump of sea which hampers a small vessel. During the four trips which Susan and I have now made along this chain we have never found conditions quite the same; sometimes we have lain becalmed for hours until we realized we would not reach an anchorage before nightfall unless we motored; at others we

▶

13. Port Gustavia, St. Barts, where rum costs only 3*s*. 6*d*. a bottle and whisky 12*s*., is centre of the West Indies smuggling trade. Through a week of bad weather we shared the harbour with cruising yachts from Canada, Turkey, and the U.S.A.

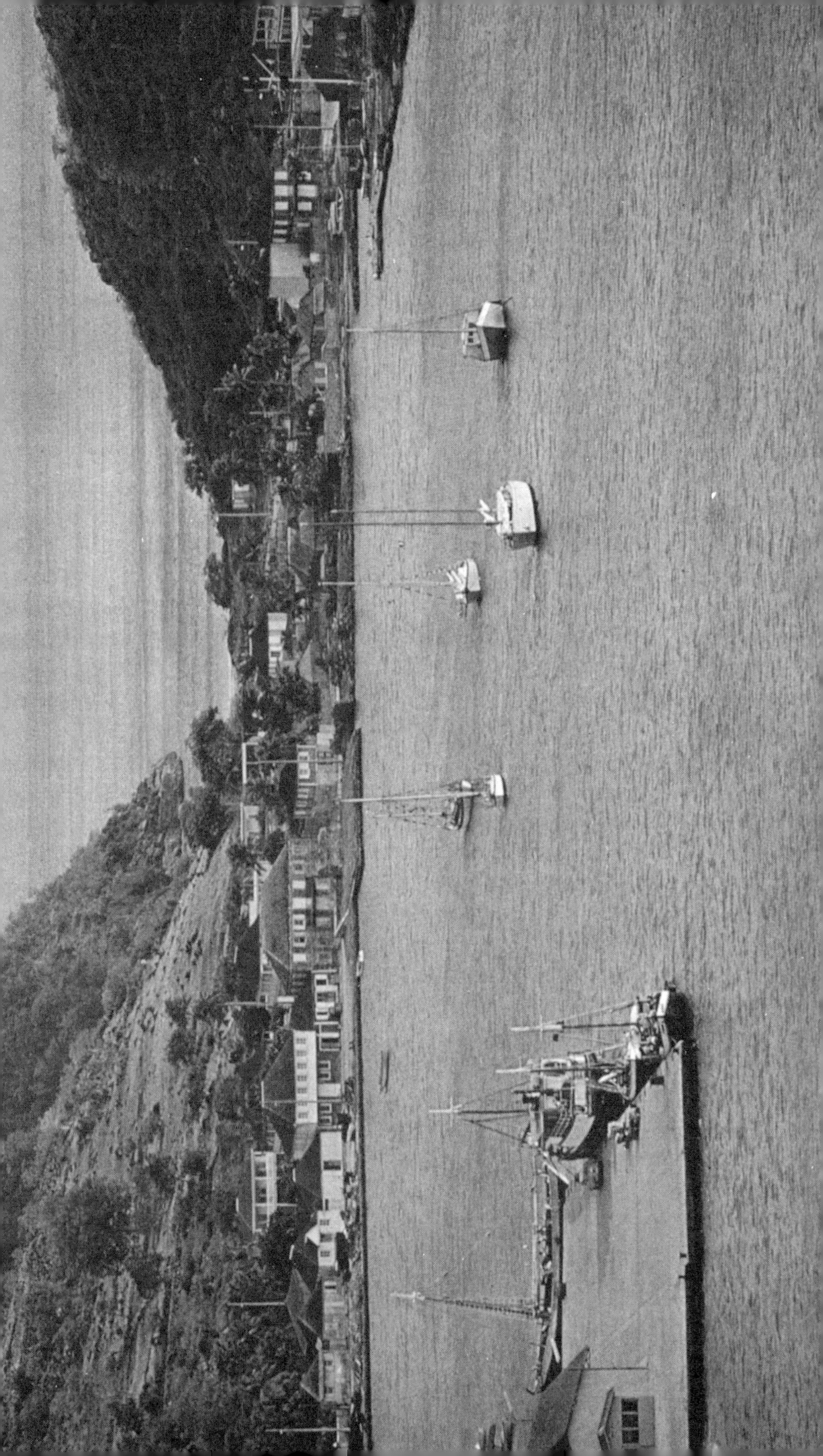

have sailed right through a high island's lee with only a few minutes of fluky winds. Opinions as to the best procedure for a sailing vessel differ, but we now favour keeping within a mile or so of the shore, and this at least has the advantage that one can enjoy the magnificent scenery at close quarters. In the channels between the islands one is, of course, fully exposed to the trade wind and the open Atlantic; there the going can be rugged, but we have never found the sea as rough as we had expected it to be with 3,000 miles of open ocean to windward. These channels are mostly less than 30 miles wide, and it is fun for a few hours to have the ship hard-pressed under full sail with the spray flying in the sunshine and the lee scuppers spouting, conditions which if there was far to go would be considered intolerable. One of the inter-island passages which can be awkward is that between Deshayes Bay in Guadeloupe and English Harbour in Antigua, for this is a distance of 40 miles, and as Antigua lies a little out of line with the other islands, often one is hard on the wind when heading for it from the south. Also, the entrance to English Harbour is not easy for the stranger to identify until it is close, and if he falls to leeward of it he will have a hard job reaching it before dark because of the lee-going current, and it is not lighted.

Each of the islands offers one or more anchorages on the lee side. Most of these are in open bays, but in the winter it is rare indeed for the wind to blow from any but a north-east to south-east direction, so usually one lies comfortably enough. St. Lucia, however, has two good landlocked harbours; Marigot, tucked in behind a palm-fringed spit which hides it from seaward, is a dark green pool with steep, tree-clad slopes on three sides; and Vigie Cove, which leads out of Castries Harbour and lies beside the attractive airport.

It was for the latter that we headed to see if the yard there, which we had been told employed the only reliable engineer north of Grenada, could put right our defective motor. The

◀

14. Inter-island sloops and schooners lie in Anguilla's roadstead off the village of Sandy Ground, waiting for their cargoes of salt, which is obtained by evaporation from sea-water ponds, one of which can be seen in the foreground.

firm had been started by Bert and Grace Ganter; they had reclaimed a swamp, built a quay, and erected on it a number of buildings to house workshops, stores, and tools. But Bert became ill and had to return to England before the buildings got their roofs, and his wife was bravely keeping the place going while the rain lay in puddles round her and the tools rusted. Her engineer Sputnik—he was a clever boy, but slow of movement—diagnosed big-end trouble, and in view of the fact that the motor was old, and that later on we would need power through 1,000 miles of inland waterway, we thought it best to obtain a new one while at an island which had good connections with the U.K. A Geeste Line ship sails each week from Barry to Castries; in response to our cable Stuart Turner had the new motor packed and on the dock at Barry ready to be loaded aboard the ship due to sail that week; but she, apparently without saying a word to anyone, sailed two days early and left behind what we considered to be the most important item on her manifest. However, we did not know about this until later, for in the meantime we had sailed north to do our refit.

As the terms Greater and Lesser Antilles and Windward and Leeward Islands have changed their meanings over the years and caused some confusion, perhaps a word of explanation might not be out of place here. Today the Greater Antilles comprise the big islands (Cuba, Jamaica, Hispaniola, and Puerto Rico) which extend from the Gulf of Mexico to the eastward. The rest of the islands right down to Grenada are known as the Lesser Antilles, and these in turn are split into Windward Islands (Grenada to Martinique) and Leeward Islands (those north of Martinique). When sailing among the Lesser Antilles a minor but recurring irritation to the cruising man is the need to enter and clear his vessel at each island, no matter whether he has only come from and is bound for another of the same nationality. We found it worth while to type a number of crew lists, leaving blank the date and port, for at least two are required at each island. Unless there is another yacht at the anchorage able to tell one the correct procedure, it is impossible to know whether to remain aboard until the officials come off or to go ashore and call on them. In some places they never come off, at others they are angry if you go ashore, and at a few places—Castries, capital of St. Lucia, is one of these—the officials can be downright disobliging. But Castries is notoriously a bad place in other ways; many yachts have been robbed there, both by day and by night; the urchins at the landing blackmail you into paying to have the dinghy 'minded', and shout abuse if you decline; and most of the shop assistants prefer to sell nothing rather than bother to look for what you want. The contrast in the French islands is remarkable; there the people have more pride, dress better, and are cheerful, and the slight formalities are a pleasure rather than a burden.

In day sails we made our way north, and a week before Christmas came in past fortified Barclay Point to the perfect shelter of English Harbour, where many yachts were lying, some alongside the dockyard, others at anchor. Among them were several old friends: *Northern Light* and *Rose Rambler* (last met in the Canaries), *Widgee* and *Valfreya* (last met at Madeira), and *Alano* (we last saw her many years ago at Gibraltar). It was like coming home, and there ashore to welcome us were Vernon and Emmie Nicholson, and Tom and Ann Worth (of round-the-world *Beyond* fame), who were having a house built.

The fourteen years which had passed since our last visit had brought some changes. Most of the old buildings now have roofs; the pay office in which the Nicholsons had lived for many years is now a shop and radio station, and the Nicholsons have moved to the powder magazine, which they have converted into an intriguing home—the bath is of transparent plastic and beneath it a flood-lit coral garden, so that as you lie in it you can easily imagine that at any moment a crab may nip your stern or a sea-urchin spine penetrate. Ditches had been dug in the dockyard and cables were being laid, for very soon *Son et Lumière* was to come to the old place. The engineers' quarters are now an inn, the officers' quarters are inhabited by the wives and children of some of the charter-fleet skippers, and the Admiral's House is a museum. Even electricity has arrived, but that rare Antiguan commodity, fresh water, is still in short supply, for the rainwater cisterns used in Navy days do not appear to hold enough for the present inhabitants; while we were there the main was turned on only for one hour a day, and the trickle that materialized was not of high quality.

Having made our number with our friends, we took *Wanderer* to the far end of Commissioners Bay, where, close under the weather shore, there was not a ripple on the water to interfere with our topside painting operations, and we had ideal conditions, with never even a shower of rain, in which to do our refit. We worked all the daylight hours for a week, and then joined in the Christmas festivities, which started with a special edition of 'Children's Hour', the title given to the period starting at 0900, when by radio the Nicholsons talk with their charter yachts. This is always an interesting affair, ranging from urgent messages and instructions to pure farce, such as when almost the entire fleet became involved in the recovery of a bathing wrap which someone thought she had left on a beach. Vernon conducted the programme on Christmas morning, and it consisted entirely of nonsense poems, one for every yacht away from port. That night we dined in *Alano*'s cockpit with Fred and Joan Georgeson—Americans who had gone to England to have their ship designed and built, and now were chartering—and this was followed by a party at the powder magazine; seventy people were invited, and a hundred turned up. There the living-room floor is of planks laid and payed like a deck, and is provided with scuppers so that it can be washed down; that is, of course, if there is any water.

Most of the yachts and their people we expected to see again some time, but not the Cordiner family in *Valfreya*, as they were to sail direct for Panama and the Pacific. It was some months later that we had news of the disaster which befell them. They made their way without incident to Panama and for 4,000 miles out into the Pacific, but then one dark night ran aground on the windward reef of an uninhabited atoll, one of the Tuamotu, a group of low islands which once again had justified its other name—the Dangerous Archipelago. *Valfreya* was a total loss, but somehow the family managed to get ashore, where they lived on coconuts for three days. Then the chief of a neighbouring atoll while out fishing saw their signals, and took them to his island, where they were guests for several weeks until a schooner called and carried them to Tahiti.

Before sailing we shipped a third hand, a six-weeks-old black-and-white kitten from the powder magazine, and we christened him Nicholson. Ann Worth, who knows about cats, went into St. Johns and bought a deep bread-bin (to be used as a sand box) and a supply of canned cat food called Paws; the other well-known brand called Kitty-Kat was not available as the locals had bought it all to eat themselves in preference to the more expensive corned beef. Thus prepared we headed south.

The winter trade wind was by now fully established and blowing hard, and the sea was rough. As soon as we were clear of the harbour mouth we felt the full force of it, and with the wind on the beam *Wanderer* lurched with dizzy swoops to leeward. Nicholson, who had been staggering around like a drunk, neatly vomited his breakfast on to the cabin floor, and then turned in in his basket at the foot of the mast and went to sleep. From that day on he has taken everything except cows and small children in his stride, and has never again been seasick. I wish I could get my sea-legs as quickly and completely as that. Most of the inter-island passages we took with a reef in the mainsail, and four days of hard daylight sailing brought us to Vigie Cove, but only to learn of the shipping delay to our new motor. We did not want to stop for a week there in the rain—it always rains when we are at Vigie—so we hurried back north to Martinique, because at Fort de France, capital of that island, there is a slip, and we wanted to haul out so as to patch the copper sheathing on the waterline at the stem, where it had eroded and become perforated, before the worm got in.

The procedure at Fort de France is to go to the air-conditioned offices of Pan American and ask for Mlle Grant, who works there. This charming woman is the daughter of the owner of the boatyard which has the slip, and she speaks English. She quickly understood our needs, spoke into a telephone for a few moments, and then said:

'If you will please go tomorrow morning at eight to the big buoy at the far end of the docks, a pilot will meet you to show you the way.'

This we did. We followed the pilot over the shallows, and an hour later were safely hauled out under the trees—I had never believed the story that some yards use padded boathooks when handling smart yachts, but now I know it is true. The copper was patched, the bottom was antifouled—the yard hands who helped us with this even cleaned our brushes without being asked—and a day later we were afloat once more. When we called on Mlle Grant to pay the bill she said that we were to pay only two-thirds of it, and when we asked why this should be she replied:

'My father always cuts the cost for people that he likes', meaning, perhaps, those not engaged in chartering.

If you go barefoot, as we do, you will know how hateful it is when some visitor from the shore brings a little sand aboard on his shoes. Imagine, then, living in *Wanderer* with Nicholson. He knew quite well what the sand box was for, but he also regarded it as a play-pen in which to dig, and his little pink pads, a bit damp at times, carried the sharp grit all over the ship, so that soon the brightwork looked as though it had been rubbed down with coarse glasspaper. The Carrs in *Havfruen III*, who have a pair of Siamese, suggested we try wood planings, and a final gesture of the kind Grants was to present us with a sailbag full of sweet-smelling cedar planings. Fortunately Nicholson approved of this and used it for its intended purpose.

Then back we went to Vigie Cove for the third time. The motor had arrived, the customs had been placated, and within a day it had been installed by Sputnik. One last cool bath we had in Grace Ganter's shower-house (this being a substantial concrete building, it is here that she takes shelter when there is a hurricane warning) and we felt a little sad as we left her at the yard, waving from her roofless buildings as we headed north.

This time we succeeded in *sailing* through the lee of the high islands, and a few days later returned to English Harbour. The charter yachts had thinned out a bit by now, but there were several genuine cruisers in port, and among them we were fortunate to make friends with the Greys—bearded Chuck and his lovely blonde wife Chris—in the steel centreboard cutter *Altair*. They had sailed from Chicago two years before and took the great-circle course from Nova Scotia to England; they reached the Mediterranean by way of canals, had recently crossed the Atlantic in the trade wind, and now were homeward bound. We were to see more of this delightful couple from then on, and at times to cruise in company with them.

The trenches in the dockyard had now been filled in, an auditorium had been excavated at the far side of the harbour, and the first performance of *Son et Lumière* was to be that night. We intended to go and buy tickets at $5.00 BWI each, but we had a nice young couple bound for New Zealand to supper, and the show, to which the Administrator and other important people had been invited, had started before we were ready. So we rowed over to the stone quay near Clarence House, which is now the Administrator's week-end residence, and strolled up the hill towards it in the starlight to see what was to be seen. In front of the old house stands a flagstaff on a ha-ha, and there we seated ourselves with the audience of 1,000 at our feet, watching the dockyard buildings come to life as the changing coloured lights played on them, and listening to the sound effect and dialogue. Two policemen stood behind us, also getting a free show. Presently there came a point in the performance when there was a ball at Clarence House, and Nelson and Mrs. Nisbet were sitting out. Slowly we became bathed in intensifying blue light. The policemen with great presence of mind dropped to the ground and rolled over and over until they were out of sight. Our reactions were slower, and then it was too late.

'Pretend to be a shrub,' Susan whispered between clenched teeth.

We sat motionless and embarrassed with, we supposed, the eyes of the audience on us for what seemed like hours, until our lights faded and those at the dockyard over the water came on. Afterwards we learnt that our presence had not gone unnoticed, but that it was thought we were an intended part of the performance. We found the show impressive and at times moving, but the fact is that although Nelson was there as captain of H.M.S. *Boreas* for three years, his stay was an unhappy and uneventful one, and English Harbour has no very interesting history; without that it is difficult to make an effective *Son et Lumière*.

Some people do not like English Harbour now that it has become commercialized, but Susan and I thought it was good fun, and we left with some regret when we sailed early in February for Port Gustavia, the free port on the French island of St. Barthélémy (St. Barts). We made a gentle overnight passage, the high islands to port of us standing out bold and black in the moonlight, and our only anxiety was that Nicholson, who was making his first attempts to climb the rigging, might tumble overboard, for he could get no proper grip on the antichafe plastic tubing in which the lower parts of the shrouds are encased. Dawn was clear and orange-tinted, but as we approached St. Barts, which had been clearly visible for some time, a pall of blue-black cloud rapidly spread from the north, bringing torrents of rain and a strong wind. We groped our way into the little harbour, and there remained weather-bound for a week with three other yachts, a Canadian, a Turk, and our American friend *Altair*, while squalls in excess of 40 knots whipped the water white and coated the deck with salt. As rum costs only 3*s*. 6*d*. a bottle there, and whisky 12*s*., there was, naturally enough, a party aboard one or other of the yachts each evening. St. Barts is getting a few tourists now, but I believe its main income still comes, as it has in the past, from the smuggling trade, for this is the place to which the schooners come to load their cargoes of spirits and carry them off to other islands; it is said that some of the rum distilled in Barbados and shipped in bond to St. Barts is smuggled back to its island of origin, and a profit is made. On the south side of the harbour facing the town there stands a 'yacht club', founded and run by Miles Reincke, an obliging German who will get you almost anything you want at the same prices as rule in the shops. We wanted to buy a Zenith radio receiver here, but Reincke, who was not an agent for it, tried hard but without success to sell us another kind for which he was an agent, and then heaped coals of fire on our heads by giving us a superb dinner in his home. All the time we were at St. Barts, and in spite of the high wind, American, Canadian, and British courtesy ensigns were flown at the club flagstaff, and as Reincke did not have a Turkish ensign—after all, one does not expect to see a Turkish yacht in these waters—he spelt out the word TURKEY in international code flags instead.

After making a one-night stop at the next island, St. Martin, which, curiously, is half French half Dutch, we came to near-by Anguilla, which since our visit has created quite a stir by seceding from the State of St. Kitts and determining to run her own affairs as a dependency directly under the Mother Country, to which she is very loyal. We had a hard beat along the north coast of this low, flat island, and anchored off the village of Sandy Ground in company with a dozen trading vessels, schooners and sloops, most of which looked a bit the worse for wear. Although Anguilla was trying in a simple way to attract the tourist to her fine sandy beaches, she seemed to be having little success, and relied for her livelihood mostly on remittance money sent by Anguillians living abroad, and on the export of 150 tons of salt a month. Just inshore of the beach at Sandy Ground is a large seawater pond; there in the summer salt from the evaporated water is scraped together, and built into a stack from which it is later bagged and loaded into the coasters, almost the entire operation being done by hand. Unfortunately the last hurricane had destroyed the best pond, and the cost of rebuilding the dikes is too great to be undertaken without outside help.

Now only 80 miles to the west of us lay the archipelago of the British and American Virgins, and this was something to which we had been looking forward ever since we first thought of cruising there, and the nearer we got the more highly was it spoken of by sailing people. We were not disappointed; indeed, we think that archipelago provides one of the most pleasant

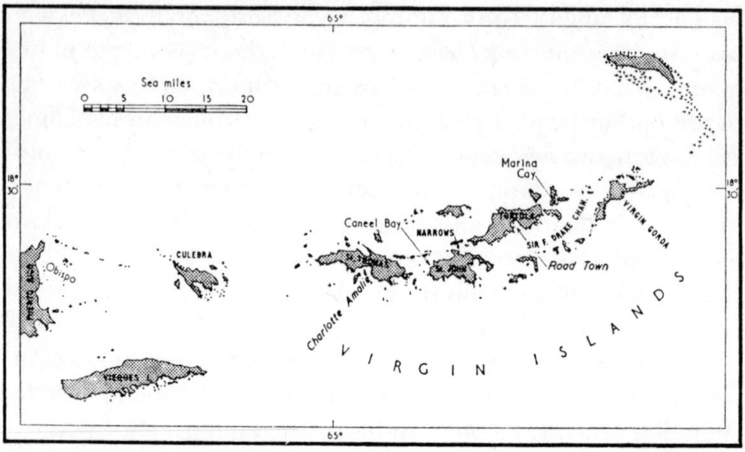

BRITISH AND AMERICAN VIRGIN ISLANDS

little cruising areas that we know. For the most part the islands are high and there are many attractive and sheltered anchorages among them; pilotage, though interesting, is not difficult or dangerous, and Sir Francis Drake Channel and The Narrows (this separates British from American territory) are so well sheltered by the enclosing islands that to sail upon them is like sailing over some inland sea transported out into the wastes of the Atlantic. There is variety to be had there, too. Some of the islands are uninhabited, and one can lie in their coves in solitude and silence; in fact, we were doing just that in Virgin Gorda Sound one day, at anchor in the lee of a tiny islet, when Sten and Brita Holmdahl's immaculate *Fjording* came in and anchored near. Their charterers from the U.S.A. were kind and understanding people, so we were invited aboard that evening. We found Sten and Brita unchanged, except that Sten now spoke English, and while we sat in low chairs on the quarter-deck under the awning, drinking our cool rum punches in the latticed light shed by a swinging basket lamp, Sten fired up his gas and charcoal barbecue and cooked us steaks. With touching tact their guests said they were tired, and turned in early, leaving the four of us with lights extinguished to talk over old times.

Then there are the more sophisticated places, Marina Cay, for example, a tiny, peaked island set on a crescent of coral reef which, extending both ways, gives good shelter to its anchorage. On this Allan and Jean Batham, who had set out some years before to sail in *Falcon* to Vancouver, B.C., had settled and built cottages, and now run the most popular open club in the islands, with accommodation for thirty guests. We found a contrast in Caneel Bay on the American Island of St. John, where a chalet hotel has been built in well-groomed surroundings; when we landed to post some letters we felt (quite wrongly) that every footstep might cost a dollar. Finally there are the capitals: Road Town in Tortola for the British Virgins, and Charlotte Amalia in St. Thomas for the American Virgins. The contrast is remarkable. Road Town is small, sleepy, and mighty inefficient, and is sited at one of the worst anchorages in the group; yet it has a certain charm. Charlotte Amalie is a roaring, bustling place where the streets are jammed with the immensely long, low cars which we had seen advertised in American magazines, and until then had thought existed only in the perverted minds of advertising agents' artists. Sometimes in one day two big cruise liners pour their people in to add to the congestion. Air-conditioned supermarkets offer acres of neatly packaged foods, which look such fun in the colour pictures on the cartons, but often taste of nothing, and pour syrupy music over the shoppers as they wheel their stainless steel carriers along the hypnotic aisles. They say you can buy anything in St. Thomas, but this, we found, does not include navigational requirements; the harbourmaster, who is agent for U.S. charts, had not bothered to obtain for us the *Nautical Almanac* or any of the charts for which we had asked months in advance. But we shall never forget the gathering of characterful yachts in the anchorage and at the marina, or the people, again mostly married couples, who run them. Among them was the Norgroves' *White Squall*, aboard which we spent a memorable evening. Ross was just the same, full of fun and vitality as he played his guitar and sang for us the songs we had first heard along Tahiti's waterfront; Doreen was a little greyer of hair and perhaps a trifle worn by the almost constant grind of shopping for food in the few short hours between one charter and the next, and by the cooking and serving of gourmet meals. It was, perhaps, appropriate that the Southern Cross, though low in the sky, should hang clear above the horizon for all of us to see that night.

After our first visit to St. Thomas we retraced our course back to the British Virgins just for the pleasure of sailing in smooth water in such delightful surroundings. Then, heading to the west once more, we spent a night at Culebra, a quiet island with an excellent natural harbour set in the midst of danger and forbidden areas imposed by the U.S. Navy, and then visited an island called Obispo (so small that there is no sign of it on the British charts) off the east coast of Puerto Rico. To our surprise we found a modern, American-style marina there; rows of concrete piers stuck out from the shore, each tight packed both sides with gleaming white sport fishermen—high-speed power yachts with chairs and rods arranged for big-game fishing—and some of the piers were beneath a roof so that the rods and radio antenna had to be lowered or housed to enable the vessels to get in and under out of the sun. Presumably sport fishing is a week-end pastime among Puerto Ricans, or perhaps the possession of one of these vessels is a status symbol, for although we remained two days in the middle of the week we never saw one of the huge fleet get under way.

As we sailed slowly with little wind along the north coast of Puerto Rico, Susan said:

'I've enjoyed our time among the West Indies, and all those nice people we met, but I don't think I would want to continue cruising there, lovely though the islands are.'

'Not enough excitement?' I queried.

'Perhaps it's that. Once you've been there I believe you could cruise without a log or compass, and probably even without a chart. Could almost become monotonous.'

'Well, the Bahamas should be a bit of a change,' I said. 'To judge by the charts, there's some pretty tricky pilotage there in all that shallow water, and always the chance of a norther to stir things up.'

On approaching San Juan harbour, a wicked squall of wind and rain rushed upon us, just as we were coming in to the passage between the frowning ramparts of Fort Morro and a sinister wreck on which the swell, yellow with churned-up mud, was breaking angrily. Then through the rain we saw our friend *Altair* beating out and plunging heavily in the confused sea, which now and then hid her black-and-white hull from us. She came close, then turned and led the way to an anchorage between the Club Nautico and the airport.

That evening during dinner aboard *Altair* I asked the Greys what they thought of San Juan.

'The old part of the town's cute,' said Chris from her Dutch-tiled galley, where she was brewing coffee, 'and it's worth going by bus to look at it; but it's full of tourists and it smells.'

'And watch out for theft here,' put in Chuck. 'We had our outboard stolen, *and* while we were actually on board; they cut the dinghy's painter so she blew away right down the harbour, and we were lucky to get her back. But we'll never see that motor again, and I had to buy another.'

We discussed our plans for cruising from south to north through the Bahamas, and decided to leave together in two days' time, we to head for Grand Turk (the south-easternmost of the group) and they for Caicos, 20 miles beyond, where we hoped to meet up with them again.

'How would it be if I call you by radio each day?' asked Chuck. 'Could tell you where we are and any other news.'

'That would be fun,' said Susan. 'Of course, we can't reply, but we ought to be able to pick you up on our Zenith so long as you don't get too far ahead.'

'O.K. then. I'll call you each day at noon on 2174 kilocycles and give you all the local gossip.'

5

BAHAMAS

The direct course from San Juan to Grand Turk, having crossed the great chasm of the Puerto Rico Trench, leads over the Silver Bank, a submarine plateau which rises abruptly from depths of between 1,000 and 2,000 fathoms. Over most of the bank's 500 square miles there are depths of from 10 to 20 fathoms, but here and there lie isolated rock dangers, and along its windward edge stands a forest of shallow coral heads, ready to rip the bottom out of any vessel foolish enough or unfortunate enough to come among them. There is nothing to mark this terrible danger except some breakers, and on it lie many wrecks, including five galleons of a large Spanish treasure-carrying fleet which, under the command of Vice-Admiral Gonzales, foundered there during a hurricane in 1642. Only a small part of their treasure has been recovered, and it is believed that gold and silver with a present-day value of nearly four million pounds still lie there.

However, as we had no intention of going treasure-hunting in that wild and desolate graveyard of ships, and having regard to the west-setting current in its vicinity, we and the Greys laid our courses for a point 40 miles to the north-east of the bank; from that point we could steer more directly for our respective destinations. The distance to Grand Turk by that route would be about 370 miles.

Much to our surprise the two yachts, although so different in size and type—*Altair* being a beamy, 36-foot centreboard cutter drawing only 3 feet with her board up, and *Wanderer* a narrow 30-foot sloop drawing 5¾ feet—were so evenly matched in the moderate quartering wind that they were within sight of one another all the first day, and we could see *Altair*'s masthead light through most of the night.

Although the weather was fine the sky had a smeary, threatening aspect, and when Chuck spoke to us by radio on the second day out he reported that Nassau marine operator was giving warnings of the approach of a norther. This is a winter phenomenon, an outbreak of cold, high-pressure air that interrupts the normal easterly flow of warm air. Typically it starts with the wind veering to south and south-west, and then as the cold front arrives the wind shifts suddenly to north-west and north, and may blow with gale force for some hours or for more than a day. As northers often arrive without any warning from the barometer, and sometimes without being forecast, they can be dangerous to vessels in the Bahamas, where many of the recognized anchorages are protected only from winds with an easterly component.

Altair's noon position was a little to the east of ours, and as by now we reckoned we were clear of Silver Bank, we altered course for the north end of Grand Turk, but that night the wind fell so light that we only ghosted along at less than 2 knots. *Altair* wisely took the opportunity to do a little motoring, for next day at noon we heard Chuck's deep voice say:

'*Altair* to *Wanderer! Altair* calling *Wanderer III!* We rounded the north end of Turk two hours ago in rain, and are now heading for South Caicos. Over and out.'

Our noon position that day, a somewhat questionable morning position line crossed by a bearing of the radio beacon on Turk, placed us only 15 miles from the latter. But we were now sailing in rain, which much reduced the visibility, so it was not until well on in the afternoon that we sighted the water tower, which is the most conspicuous object on the island. The rain, as usual, interfered with the wind, bringing it round from east to north, and we doubted if the Turk anchorage, which is in a crack in the fringing reef on the island's western side, would be tenable, while Caicos was too far off to be reached by us in daylight. So we hove-to and remained so through the night. The wind did not blow hard, and by dawn had veered to north-east, so we let draw, rounded Turk's northern end and coasted down its lee towards the anchorage. But although we had experienced only the weak tail-end of the norther, it must have been blowing hard farther north, for quite a large swell was coming from that direction, and it looked ugly as it ran along the shore and then swung in to smash upon it in a smother of foam and with a roar which we could hear all too clearly. One look at the anchorage with its heavy breakers was enough for us, and we bore away for Cockburn Harbour in South Caicos. As we approached that island, which lies at the eastern edge of wide and shallow Caicos Bank, but while it was still below the horizon, we could clearly see the 'bank blink', the pale green reflection of the shallow water in the atmosphere above; this sometimes enables the presence of a bank or lagoon to be discovered while still at a great distance, as we had learnt while among the atolls of the South Pacific. We entered the harbour in the afternoon without difficulty, and anchored near *Altair*. The holding ground is said to be poor, but Chris had a look through her glass-bottomed bucket and saw that our plough anchor had properly dug in. That evening the two ships' companies had a get-together, and from that time on whenever we shared an anchorage with the Greys, always the evening drinks, and sometimes the evening meal, were had by all hands in one ship or the other. It says much for the charm and tact of the Greys that we were able to do this night after night and always with renewed pleasure, and Susan and I know of few things more heartening and enjoyable than cruising strange waters in such efficient and entertaining company.

Although Turks and Caicos are farther out (from Nassau) than any other of the 'out' islands, geographically they form a part of the Bahamas group. However, they are not real Bahamas, having been a dependency of Jamaica since 1874; therefore a yacht entering there must enter again at her next island in the group, though nobody seems to take this very seriously. We ▸

15. Marina Cay, one of the smallest of the British Virgins, is set on a crescent of coral reef, which gives good shelter to the anchorage. The Bathams have built cottages on the island, and run it as a popular open club.

found dusty, wind-whipped South Caicos a cheerful but primitive little place, with many of its 800 inhabitants, who are mostly engaged in conch and lobster fishing, living in tumbledown wood and corrugated-iron shacks; we wondered what some readers of realtors' advertisements might think of this as their 'hide-away island in the sun'. However, it does have an air-strip (aviators are advised to watch for stray animals when landing) and an inn which offers special rates to customers who catch their own food.

Among the Bahamas much of one's sailing is of necessity done in the shallow water over the huge banks which extend for hundreds of square miles, where it is necessary to judge by the colour how deep the water is, and where coral heads or sand bores are dangerously near the surface; they say it takes eighteen months to become adept at this. Although we were no strangers to pilotage by eye, for the most part our experience had been gained in the Pacific and Indian Ocean, where usually the water is deep between the heads, and the dangers are easily seen. But our crossing of the Caicos Bank (see inset chart on page 71) was to be our first introduction to shoal-water sailing of this kind, so we took with us as pilot nineteen-year-old Laniel, a member of the crew of *Love Vine*, a local trading sloop which was also about to make the crossing. The passage across the bank directly from our anchorage at Cockburn was too shallow for us, though not for *Altair* and *Love Vine*, so we had to go back out into deep water and come on to the bank farther south. That was the most frightening part of the expedition, and until we had passed Six Hill Cays there were many coral heads to be avoided and because of the weed on the sea-bed they were not easy to distinguish, while to touch one would probably have been disastrous because of the swell. But once we had come properly on to the bank there was no swell and little sea. For the whole of our fast 50-mile run to

◀

16. Wind-whipped South Caicos, one of the most southerly and least-visited islands of the Bahama group, is not a true Bahama but a dependency of Jamaica. Many of its 800 inhabitants live in tumbledown shacks and are engaged in conch and lobster fishing.

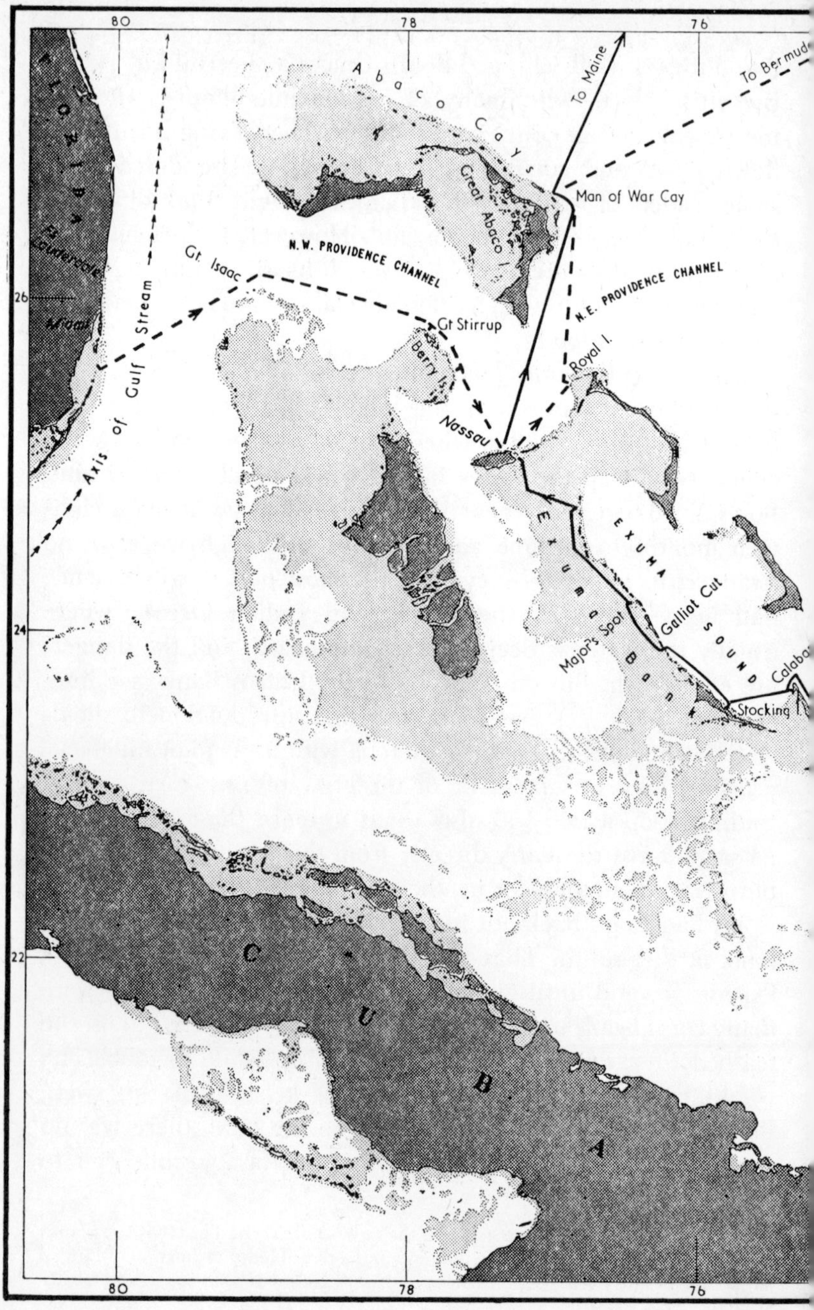

BAHA

With larger-scale i

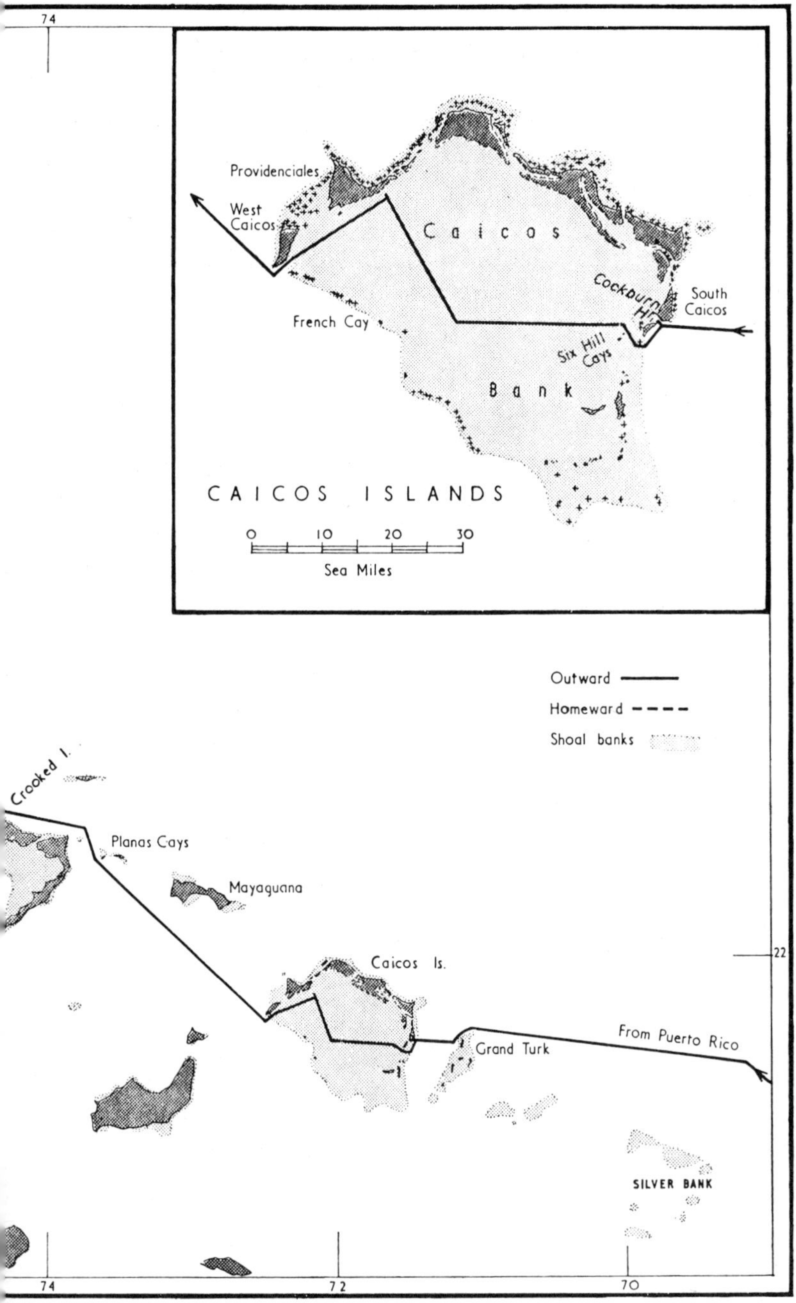

NDS

Bank and Islands

Providenciales, an island at the north-west edge of the bank, we could see *Wanderer*'s shadow on the bottom, for there was rarely more than 6 feet, and sometimes less than 6 inches, under her keel, and for most of the time we were out of sight of above-water land, as the Caicos Islands, like all the Bahamas, are low. Only occasionally did we see the distant white sails of *Altair* (she, too, had taken a pilot) and the grey ones of *Love Vine*, for those vessels with their shoal draught were able to cut a corner a long way to the north of us, while we had to steer west until we sighted tiny French Cay before turning north.

I had set the approximate course on the grid compass, but it soon became clear that Laniel had no faith in compasses; he appeared to steer by the clouds over the islands, and long before we were due to raise French Cay he became anxious—he had probably never taken this route before—and repeatedly climbed aloft to look for it, and when eventually he did sight its low scrub vegetation, an enormous white grin split his hitherto gloomy face.

Wanderer's draught of 5¾ feet is certainly too much for care-free sailing in Bahamian waters, and we found it barred some of the snugger anchorages to her. One of the difficulties of bank sailing is that night may fall before a sheltered anchorage can be reached, and as Laniel said:

'A lot of boats get sink sailing night-time.'

It has often been said that one can anchor anywhere on the banks if benighted, but this might not be safe for a vessel as small as ours because of the short, steep sea which a fresh wind can raise.

The south shore of Providenciales is marked on the chart only by a dotted line, indicating lack of topographical information, and we had expected to find there an anchorage in the lee of some cays. But the land bore no relation to the chart, and as there was insufficient water for us behind the only cay we could

▶

17. *Left:* All the way across Caicos Bank we could see *Wanderer*'s shadow on the bottom, for there was rarely more than 6 feet, and sometimes less than 6 inches, under her keel. *Right:* 'A lot of boats get sink sailing night-time,' said Laniel, our young pilot, as he steered us across 50 miles of the bank.

find, we had to anchor out in the open. Laniel lived on Providenciales, so we dropped him there well pleased with his fee of $10 and a present of chocolate, cigarettes, and a photograph of *Wanderer*, and next day sailed on our own across the rest of the bank and, with sighs of relief, out into deep water south of West Caicos, where the pointer of the echo-sounder moved from 4 to 50 fathoms in ten seconds. *Altair* had been able to take another short cut, and so got ahead of us; she was bound for Mayaguana, while we intended to make a night passage direct to Crooked Island, 170 miles away.

Information about the currents in the deep-water passages between the islands is scanty, but in this particular area the *Pilot* states that generally it sets south-west. However, as we had no wish to be set towards Mayaguana in the dark, and to be absolutely safe, or so I thought, I allowed for a 1-knot current setting in the opposite direction when deciding on the course to steer. The night was black and wild, with a strong north-east wind and rough sea, and we spent a part of it hove-to; but when at dawn we saw ahead the sinister grey line of the unlit and uninhabited Planas Cays standing astride our course, we realized that we had been set 15 miles ahead of our reckoning, and that the current, instead of setting south-west, had been running at more than 2 knots in a northerly direction. If I had acted on the information given in the *Pilot*, we would almost certainly have run ashore during the hours of darkness and would probably have lost our ship.

But a wayward current is not the only difficulty associated with pilotage among the Bahamas. The lights are few and far between, and, except along the main shipping routes, are mostly of low power and are not entirely reliable. The patent log is useless, because its rotator is so often fouled by weed, of which there are large patches floating on the sea, so the distance run must be guessed. Also, the charts are inaccurate in many

◀

18. *Top: Altair* and *Wanderer* share a strange and lonely berth at French Wells, where there is no visible land to windward of them. *Bottom:* In the foreground is one of the creeks which wind their way into the heart of Crooked Island. Young mangroves stand like twigs along the sandbanks.

respects; for example, during our time among the islands we anchored on two occasions in the lee of islands which are not shown at all, and on one occasion we sailed over the top of others which are shown, but which obviously do not exist; in general the British charts of the area are on too small a scale to be of much use except as a guide to the course to steer from one island group or bank to the next. However, there is one publication which is of the greatest value to the visitor—indeed, I believe he could make do with this alone—a remarkable little book called *Yachtsman's Guide to the Bahamas* and published by the Ministry of Tourism, Nassau. This describes almost every anchorage and passage, and it contains a wealth of excellent chartlets, sketches, and local information which are the results of many years of patient labour by its originator, the British artist the late Harry Etheridge in his yacht *Grebe*, and the present editor, Harry Kline.

Although we sailed fast and uncomfortably all day, we failed to reach an anchorage at Crooked Island before dark, so on nearing Bird Rock light at the north-west end of the island we hove-to until daylight. At breakfast-time we anchored off the beach close to the spot where many years ago the yacht *Tai-Mo-Shan* went ashore; she was stranded for two weeks, but was got off almost undamaged by the tireless efforts of her naval crew and the paid help of the islanders.

We were joined there by the Greys, who had thought little of Mayaguana, but they soon headed south along the coast to investigate the possibility of reaching the anchorage at French Wells at the south end of the island, where there is said to be a depth of only 3 feet on the bar at low water. We left our radio receiver switched on, and presently Chuck's voice came into our cabin loud and clear:

'*Altair* to *Wanderer! Altair* calling *Wanderer!* We are now at French Wells, and it sure is a dandy place. Why don't you folks come on down and join us? We'll be looking for you. Out.'

So off we went to anchor outside the bar two hours after low water. Chuck came out to us in his outboard dinghy and I went with him to sound the bar with a bamboo pole. We found that the deepest part, which was very narrow, had more water than expected, just a little under 6 feet; so we laid a marker buoy there and then cautiously, with her keel smelling the sand, brought *Wanderer* in to anchor in 2 fathoms near her consort.

This was a wild and lonely berth, yet a curiously attractive one with its pastel colours and its waders; there was no visible land to windward of us, but so shallow was the water in that direction that the wind could not kick up much sea; the tide ran strongly. To the south lay the tiny Rat and Goat Cays, and to the north the low end of Crooked Island, into which long, winding creeks made their tortuous way, sometimes staked with tree markers for the benefit of the few conch fishermen, sometimes so narrow that the bushes almost met overhead. We had no outboard, and *Altair*'s outboard dinghy was not large enough to accommodate all four of us, so she with Chuck and Chris aboard towed our dinghy with us aboard, and in that manner we penetrated several miles inland to a settlement, seeing on the way small sharks and other fish swimming under us in the shallows.

After two days in that silent, watery wilderness the two yachts left together, we retrieving our buoy as we crept over the bar; but outside we took different courses and made different anchorages on the way to Stocking Island, our next rendezvous. One of our stops was at Calabash Bay, Long Island, where we crossed some suspiciously dark patches to reach an anchorage. The scene that night was eerie. The moon shone indistinctly through the thin overcast; the shallow water in which we lay was much lighter than the sky, pale like milk over the sandy bottom; a damp wind moaned in the rigging and the glass was falling. The sky was still overcast, and the wind had shifted into the south when we left at dawn, and after four hours' sailing, as we approached the awkward eastern entrance to Elizabeth Harbour—the large area of shallow water lying between Great Exuma and Stocking Island, where the annual out-island regatta is held—down came the rain, and it was impossible among so many featureless and dimly seen cays to identify any one and find the way in. So we went round outside Stocking

Island instead and entered the harbour at the other end. Stocking Island, which is long and thin, possesses a chain of four interconnected harbours, three of which are landlocked, and *Altair* and *Wanderer* shared one of these for eight days of indifferent weather, during which the wind twice boxed the compass, and we felt wonderfully snug and smug.

When we left we had a magnificent sail north in sunshine with a fresh beam wind, and with *Altair* hard in our wake, but unable to overtake us, we romped along in deep water to windward of a line of cays for 30 miles; then we spied the little light which marks Galliot Cut (one of the many channels connecting deep Exuma Sound with shallow Exuma Bank), shot in through the cut with a sluicing fair tide, and anchored in the lee of an island which is not shown on the chart.

From that point on for 100 miles and as far as Nassau all our sailing was in comparatively smooth and shallow water in the lee of the chain of Exuma Cays, where the colouring was superb and we found some attractive anchorages; but we did have one experience which served to remind us that in spite of the glowing accounts and the colour advertisements, the Bahamas can show their teeth.

One afternoon, wishing to make an early start next morning, we anchored in the lee of Big Major's Spot, one of the many uninhabited cays which lie in such profusion in those parts, and took Nicholson for his customary run ashore. The evening was quiet and lacking colour, and the forecast promised continued good weather, so we turned in with easy minds. But at midnight we were woken by the motion, and on looking out found that the wind had freshened and veered to south-south-west, and that we were barely covered by the point of our bay. Anxiously we hung on, but the wind continued slowly to veer, and by 0300 was blowing straight in and still freshening, conditions similar to those which had put *Tai-Mo-Shan* ashore on Crooked Island. Clearly it was time to go, so we reefed the mainsail, set the second staysail, and beat out. Fortunately only 2 miles away stood one of the few navigational lights in the area, a 6-miler on Harvey Cay; towards this we made our way, and when near it we took in the staysail and hove-to to await daylight. The sky was black, and to the north and west vivid flashes of lightning sprang from it, each one showing with horrible clarity the dark patches of weed or coral, we knew not which, so close under our keel. Shortly before dawn was due the sky blackened even more, and we experienced a tremendous downpour of rain which was accompanied by a squall of great violence. Further reduction of sail was needed at once, and I turned the roller-gear handle until only a rag of canvas was left standing. I guessed the wind to be blowing at about 60 knots, but later learnt that it was recorded near by at 70 knots. Mercifully that squall did not last for long, and as it and the rain moderated the sky began to lighten, and we realized with thankfulness that dawn was at hand.

As a sheltered anchorage lay only 5 miles away round at the other side of Big Major's Spot, we decided to head for it; so as soon as it was light enough for us to see what we were doing, we bore away for the channel which leads in to it past Staniel Cay. It is a narrow channel and has a bar with a depth of only 6 feet, so it was fortunate that the sea flattened out as we approached. We could see the red-roofed church, but the white beacon, which in line with it takes one in through the deepest water, was missing, and there were patches of dark-coloured bottom we had to cross. At one time there were only 3 inches of water under our keel, but as soon as the depth increased we turned to port, and swept in past Staniel Cay Yacht Club, and were astonished to see that the pier which had looked to be in good order the previous day now lay in ruins; we dodged a rock with a beacon on it (no colour, no topmark, so we had to guess which side to pass it), crossed an entry from the ocean, where the tide ran hard, and soon reached the anchorage, which we shared with the motor cruisers which had escaped from the pier when it was blown down during the gale. That night in our cosy anchorage we slept soundly, but in the early hours Susan was awakened by a scratching on the topside near her head, and on investigating found that it was being made by Nicholson, who had fallen overboard and was just managing to stem the tide. This was not his first swim, nor was it to be his last, for by the time we reached home he had in moments of inattention or forgetfulness used up all of his nine lives, but fortunately he never expended any of them while we were under way.

Some days later we arrived at Nassau, the hub of the Bahamas on New Providence, to which produce from the out-islands is still brought in sailing craft, to be sold at the quayside market, close to which the ships from America disgorge their camera-laden passengers. Because of the prevailing wind which blows through it and the strong tidal streams that run there, Nassau harbour is a poor place for small yachts, so we moved over to the Hurricane Hole Marina on Hog Island, or Paradise Island as the travel advertisements call it. This was our first experience of life in a marina, and to say we were impressed is an understatement. The Hole is oval and can accommodate forty-five vessels, each berthed alongside a little jetty. The wide perimeter is clean and flagstoned, and lighted gently at night by lamps on cast-iron posts which look as though they came from some London street. Of course, water, electricity, and telephone can be laid on at no extra cost beyond the normal charge of 15 cents a day per foot of overall length, and there is a remarkable machine which produces a never-ending supply of ice cylinders. There are also hot, fresh showers. But what impressed us most was the peace of the place after the noise of the crowded town, with only the sigh of wind among the casuarinas which surround it, and the fact that we could safely leave the ship open and unattended while we went down town in the hourly free ferry to do our shopping. Nicholson, able to step ashore day or night whenever he wished, and with a blonde friend in the yacht next door, thought this was heaven, and the squares of sand, where palms had been planted among the flagstones, must surely have been provided by a dog- or cat-lover.

When the strong wind, which had caused the Miami–Nassau power-boat race to be postponed for four days, moderated, we said an almost tearful farewell to the Greys, for the tracks of *Altair* and *Wanderer* would separate here and perhaps might never cross again. Then we sailed for Man of War Cay, one of the chain of little islands which lie along the north-east side of Great Abaco, an overnight trip in deep water which presented no difficulty. But just as we were about to run in through Man of War North Channel on to the bank down came the rain, and the land and the marks by which we had been steering vanished. The wind was right onshore and blowing fresh, and we did not want there to be any mistake in pilotage, so we hove-to and waited, hoping the strong current would not carry us too far past the opening. Presently the rain stopped, though the sky still hung heavy and overcast, and in we went. More rain, but not enough to blind us; the seas growing steep as they felt the bottom, and breaking heavily on either side; then, quite suddenly, we came into smooth pale water, and soon after, having negotiated the extremely narrow entrance channel, which has a light and two finger-posts, so it can be used at night, anchored in Man of War's cosy East Harbour.

For a Bahama this island is remarkable in having an entirely white population, mostly descended from the Loyalists who came there at the end of the American War of Independence. To us they seemed a somewhat shy and strait-laced lot, and none appeared to smoke or drink. For many years boatbuilding had been their main industry, and good, shapely boats they still do build there along the waterfront of the flower-bedecked Settlement. It is probably the colour of its inhabitants together with their good manners and honesty, and the unspoilt nature of the island, that has caused Man of War to become a winter holiday place for a few discerning American families; today the boatbuilding industry has largely given way to the building and maintenance of simple but attractive homes for them. All round East Harbour white and green walls and roofs peep out from among the bushes, and little wooden piers (the Americans call them docks, and pronounce the word 'darks') jut out into the water.

We became friendly with several of these shore-based families who were enjoying their last few days on the island, for soon they would be returning to the States and their little houses would be shuttered for the summer. But one of our most fortunate encounters was with the Canadian yacht *Wind's Song*. George Cook had designed and built her in Nova Scotia, and now with his artistic wife Sonny, and their children Peter and Alison, lived permanently aboard and was engaged in the chartering business. In the summer they sailed out of Hackett's Cove, Nova Scotia, and in the winter out of Man of War, making the voyage south each autumn and north again in the spring. No one could quite take the place of Chuck and Chris so soon after our parting from them, but this engaging and stimulating family came very near to doing so, and many a social gathering we had with them between their chartering engagements, aboard either their ship or ours. It is meetings such as this, the folk one gets to know and love, the learning of their thoughts and aims, that make voyaging such a worthwhile occupation. George, we thought, was happy with his boat, his work, and his lovely family, but soon the children would have to go to school; meanwhile, Sonny, who is much younger than George, and does not always take too kindly to charterers, has many ambitions, among them the wish to be a poet and a nurse. The sadness at parting from people such as these leaves a wound, and although time may heal this the scar remains.

We did visit some other of the Abacos, including more sophisticated Elbow Cay, dominated by the red-and-white-striped lighthouse, which is the landfall for so many ships bound from Europe to the Gulf or Panama. But most of our time was spent at Man of War being social and preparing for the next, and probably most difficult, passage of our voyage.

▶

19. *Top:* Hurricane Hole Marina on Hog Island has a flagstoned perimeter and iron lamp-posts which look as though they came from some London street. The place is well sheltered from the prevailing winds by a fine stand of casuarinas. *Bottom:* Although the boatbuilding industry on Man of War Cay has largely given way to the building and maintenance of holiday homes, good shapely boats they still do build there along the tree-shaded waterfront of the Settlement.

6

FOG

Our intention now was to attempt to sail no'-nor'-east for almost the full length of the United States without putting in anywhere until we reached Bar Harbor, 1,200 miles away in the State of Maine, the most northerly of all the eastern states. We had discussed this plan with several knowledgeable people, some of whom had said it was still too early in the year to think of going 'down east', while others suggested it would be better to coast there, perhaps using part of the Intracoastal Waterway. But we hoped to return by that route later in the year; besides, we felt that if we did put in anywhere along the coast we might never reach Maine at all, and we particularly wanted to go there, because it is said to be the most lovely cruising area in the country, as well as the most rugged from the weather point of view, and therefore presented something of a challenge. On the way we must pass two great promontories, Cape Hatteras and Cape Cod; both are low and have dangerous shoals lying off them, and the latter is subject to 20 per cent of fog in May and June. The Gulf Stream also needed some consideration. From Florida to Cape Hatteras its axis of greatest velocity follows the general direction of the coast, and not until it reaches the Cape does it flow in a more easterly direction. Should we add 200 miles to the distance by heading for it at its closest point so as to have the benefit of a free ride of

◀

20. Man of War entrance shows the typical colouring the Bahamas pilot must understand if he is to judge where the deepest water lies. But here there are aids enabling an entry to be made by night: a little light structure on one of the entrance points, and two finger-posts standing where the channel divides. The branch running out of picture to the right leads to the Settlement, the other to East Harbour.

30–50 miles a day in the right direction; or should we ignore it and steer direct for the Nantucket Shoals lightvessel off Cape Cod, thus giving stormy Hatteras a berth of 150 miles? After much study and discussion we decided on the latter course.

We had chosen Bar Harbor as our destination because it is an official port of entry and lies as far down east as it was our intention to go, being within 50 miles of the Bay of Fundy, where the tidal range is greater than anywhere else in the world. Also, if there was fog as we approached, we might well find the radio beacon on off-lying Mount Desert Rock of some assistance. We expected that cloud or fog might often make observations of sun or stars impossible, so we would want to sight Nantucket Shoals lightvessel in order to be certain of our position before entering the Great South Channel, the passage which lies between the Georges Bank and the shoals off Cape Cod (see chart on page 92). Here again radio might be useful, as the lightvessel has a beacon with a range of 100 miles.

We left our peaceful anchorage at Man of War on 18 May, Susan's birthday, and the Cooks in *Wind's Song* kindly escorted us out to the dark blue water of the open ocean; there they gave a final wave and turned back, as they had some refitting to do and would not be starting north until June. We put *Wanderer* on course for the lightvessel 900 miles away, and it did seem strange to be heading east of north for the first time in nearly a year. We turned over the steering to Blondie, bent on the weather-cloths to keep spray out of the cockpit, and settled down to our seagoing routine.

We were fortunate with the weather to begin with, for the wind, which during the past few days had been out of the north-east, shifted to south-east on the morning of our departure, and for three days we had pleasant sailing under a blue sky with the wind just abaft the beam. We were fortunate in another respect as well, though we did not know about it then, for had we remained among the Abaco Cays for another two weeks, as some old hands who knew Maine well had urged us to do, we would have been seriously delayed by Alma, the first and very early hurricane of the season.

We were now sailing along the western edge of the Sargasso Sea, an area about which more colourful fiction has been written than about any other part of the oceans: stories of sailing ships becalmed until their crews died of starvation, and their hulls rotted, held fast in a great desert of weed and other flotsam, where giant octopuses lived, and 'slimy things did crawl with legs upon the slimy sea'. Such stories die hard, and, indeed, are still widely believed, but alas! for it might be no bad thing if there were still some mystery and a fear of the unknown in these sophisticated and scientific days, the Sargasso Sea is not like this at all, as can be vouched for by the crews of the great fleet of yachts which every other year race through part of it on their way from Newport to Bermuda, and by people making the voyage from Bermuda to the Azores. The Sargasso Sea differs from the rest of the North Atlantic only in that it is a slowly rotating eddy created by the clockwise-running currents around it, and that a great quantity of Sargassum weed, inhabited by a variety of tiny creatures which have adapted themselves to such an environment, collects there. The only real mystery is that nobody knows where the weed comes from, and the only inconvenience likely to be caused to a vessel passing through it is the fouling of her patent log rotator, and, as I have already said, we were for that reason not able to use our log until we had got north of Cape Hatteras. However, on the course we were steering that did not matter, for I was able to take the morning observation when the sun was abeam so that the resulting position line was parallel to the course; therefore any error in guessing the distance run between the morning and the noon observations had no effect on the final fix.

Three days after leaving Man of War the sky hazed over, the wind began to shift and freshen, and by the time we had reached the latitude of Hatteras was blowing at about 30 knots from ahead and with rain; there seemed no point in trying to struggle on against this, so we hove-to on the starboard tack under the close-reefed mainsail only, and waited for an improvement.

Since losing touch with the radio station at Nassau, we had

been trying to pick up some U.S. station broadcasting proper weather forecasts, but until now we had been able to receive only commercial stations—dozens of them, for nearly every town has one, most have several, and there are said to be 6,000 in the country. Every few minutes, and sandwiched in between short bursts of music, sports reports, and advertisements for all manner of interesting things, these gave odd scraps of news, the time, and the temperature outside the studio. All this, except the advertisements, came pouring out in a torrent of breathless words without so much as a pause between one subject and another, and the announcers gave not the names of their cities, but only their stations' call letters, usually wrapped up in a little jingle. It did not help us much when we heard that 'The WCAV temperature is fifty-two degrees, and tornadoes are expected in the area this afternoon', for WCAV could equally well be in Dakota or Florida—it eventually turned out to be in Philadelphia, and that was not much help, either. This was our first introduction to American commercial broadcasting, and we felt bewildered. But Susan persevered while we were lying hove-to off Hatteras, and eventually managed to pick up the Fort Macon marine operator's nasal drawl: from her we got faintly not only a marine forecast, which promised an improvement, but a Notice to Mariners, the gist of which was that a tug carrying a large steel erection to Diamond Shoal (where, we guessed, the lightvessel was being replaced with something more permanent) had in rough seas lost the whole affair overboard, and as this had occurred in comparatively shallow water, the thing constituted a hazard to inshore shipping.

After we had lain hove-to for twenty-seven hours, the wind shifted enough for us to be able to lay the course once more, and we got moving fast in a roughish sea. Though the rain had ▶

21. For several days before we reached Nantucket Shoals lightvessel the fog grew thicker. *A:* Moisture hung from the boom in elongated drops like embryo stalactites. *B:* The radar reflector was rigged up on a boathook right forward. *C:* Susan did much of the steering, while I took bearings of the lightvessel's radio beacon. *D:* When we sighted the 14-mile light it showed only as a faint glow like St. Elmo's fire high above us, and the lightvessel's hull was barely visible as we hurried by. (These shots are from our movie film.)

stopped, the sky was gloomy, and it remained so until almost the end of the passage; but just occasionally the sun showed briefly and indistinctly through the cloud, and as we were out of range of the coastal radio beacons and did not have facilities for using Consolan, which has a greater range, our navigation had to depend on snapshots of the sun at those infrequent moments. This was a little worrying, as such sights are hard to take and may be inaccurate, and opportunities are easily missed unless one is standing by with the sextant ready. But at least I thought we should be able to find the Nantucket Shoals light-vessel by radio if we could come to within 100 miles of her.

The night we crossed the axis of the now more east-going Gulf Stream the sea temperature dropped 20°F., and below deck the ship became damp with the resulting condensation; but we knew that from now on we could once more keep the butter in the bilge and find it properly refrigerated at breakfast-time. The wind, having hauled round to the south-east after the hard blow, remained there, and although this was fine for our progress we could have wished it blew from some other direction, for we had learnt that the south-easter is the wind which brings fog to the waters inshore of the Gulf Stream, where its warm damp air crosses the cold waters of the Labrador Current. And sure enough it did, and the fog grew thicker as we made northing, condensing on the sails, and hanging for a moment on the under-side of the boom in elongated drops like embryo stalactites, before blowing away to leeward.

Although Blondie had been steering all the way from Man of War, we had, of course, been keeping our ten-minute look-out for shipping, but had seen little except a few fishing vessels and U.S.S. *Corry*; she kindly came out of her way to ask if we required any assistance, and her people on the upper deck gave us a heartening cheer as she sheered off. Grey and lean, she made a fine sight as she resumed speed and arced back on to

◄

22. Cat-size Island in Long Cove, Vinalhaven. The perfect playground for Nicholson; not so large that he could get lost, not so small that there was much risk of him falling off it in a moment of inattention. *Wanderer* lies to a log mooring, a type that can survive when the cove is frozen over in the winter.

her course, leaving a swath of foam-streaked green water in her wake. But now in fog we considered it necessary for one or other of us to be on deck all the time in case a quick alteration of course to avoid collision was needed, and it was then that we began really to feel the cold. Nicholson, with superb feline balance, was indifferent to the motion, but he, too, felt chilly and spent most of his time in the bunk which Susan and I used in turn, and kept a small patch of welcome warmth waiting there for us.

At the first sign of reduced visibility we had put up the radar reflector, and as this is such a bother in the rigging, where it chafes and tears at everything within its reach, this time we rigged it on the end of the boathook which we lashed vertically to the guardrail right forward. There it was well out of the way and could not interfere with anything, but it was only 12 feet above the water and probably not high enough to be effective with much of a sea running.

The wind remained firmly at south-east, but it varied so much in strength that sometimes we hurried along under reduced sail, and at other times there was not enough wind to keep the sails asleep; but we continued to make runs of about 100 miles each day.

We were certainly greatly relieved when, during the afternoon of our ninth day at sea, the four long dashes of the radio beacon on the Nantucket Shoals lightvessel came into the headphones faint but clear at a distance, by my reckoning, of 80 miles. It had not been possible to get any sun sights for the past two days, but now we hoped to be able to home on the lightvessel by radio.

After nightfall, when we were still some 50 miles short of her, the fog closed in more thickly than ever, and our range of visibility was probably not more than 50 yards. In order to steer with the greatest possible accuracy, and to be ready for an instant alteration of course if we should meet some other vessel, we had unlatched Blondie and were steering by hand, but Susan had more steering than I, because each hour I needed to take bearings of the beacon. Apart from the red and green haze where our bow lamp tried to pierce the fog, the night was absolutely black, and there was not so much as a gleam of phosphorescent light. We were running fast with a rising wind and sea, under the reefed mainsail only. As the night wore on I took bearings more frequently, for in such thick weather it was imperative that we sight the lightvessel before altering course for the Great South Channel. The cabin was dimly lit by one gimballed lamp only, so as not to dazzle Susan, who was now doing all the steering. The rubber-cupped headphones excluded all sounds but the morse signal, with which my head seemed to be filled even during the silent periods, and I felt dizzy as I tried to steady myself against the motion and watch the swinging card of the hand-held compass on which the direction-finding aerial was mounted. Once or twice I shouted a slight alteration of course to Susan, and lifting one headphone heard her voice, clear above the noise of our progress, repeat it; in the black square of the hatchway I saw her yellow oilskinned figure illuminated for a moment as she switched on the light and bent over the compass to adjust its verge ring. Then all was dark again as she turned off the light and resumed steering by the luminous grid.

At dawn, which was late and reluctant to come, we could see how thick the fog was as we hurried on in our own small hazy world. Susan, looking very tired, was still steering while I navigated, when suddenly she glimpsed ahead something white which for a moment she thought was a breaker, but quickly recognized as a ship's bow-wave. Instantly she put the helm down, and as *Wanderer* sheered to starboard a great freighter loomed up to port, and so close that we could have counted her rivets; her upper works were barely visible in the fog. Without a sound from her siren either before or after, she swept silently by and vanished, leaving us with fast-beating hearts and a feeling of sickness in our stomachs. Quarter of an hour later, blurred and high above us, we saw a glow like St. Elmo's fire. This surprised us for a moment, until we realized that it was the lightvessel's 14-mile light. Again Susan altered course to windward. The indistinct mass of the vessel's hull appeared for a few moments, lifting on the swell as we closely crossed its bows, then quickly it and the light above it were swallowed up in the fog, and only then did we hear for the first time the vessel's powerful nautophone, such are the tricks that fog may play with sound.

This brief encounter was a dramatic one for us, and remembering our own near disaster so shortly before, we felt a pang of anxiety for the men aboard that lightvessel: how vulnerable they must feel in fog, with most of the shipping on the great circle courses between New York and Europe homing on them by radio, their only defences being their (often inaudible) fog signal, and a short-range warbling signal on the radio beacon frequency, which means:

'If you can hear this you are too darn close. Get the hell out of here.'

We now made a slight alteration of course to head for the light and whistle buoy 30 miles on in the Great South Channel, through which we must pass to reach Maine. We did not expect to see or hear the buoy, and we did not, but the Great South Channel is wide, and when by dead reckoning we felt we were fairly in it, we altered course for Mount Desert Rock 185 miles distant.

For the rest of that day we ran on at 6 knots in fog, hearing now and then, near or far, the sounds of ships groping. Our physical discomfort was added to by persistent driving rain, which streamed off the sails and found its way down our necks, and so great was the humidity that I do not believe there was anything below deck, except what was stowed in sealed cans or plastic bags, which was not damp, while trickles of water ran down the bulkheads just as though a hose had been playing on them. The cabin temperature had dropped to 44°F., even though the galley cooker was kept alight all the time. Eight months in the tropics had certainly not prepared us for this, and how crazy we were to attempt such a trip without a proper

▶

23. *Top:* Maine, a land of pink granite, dark spruce trees, and silent anchorages. *Bottom:* The Maine lobsterman often builds his own lean and swift 30-footer, powers her with some old engine picked up for a few dollars on the scrap-heap, and as he fits no silencer he can be heard for miles.

cabin heater! The watch on deck, with chattering teeth, had nothing much except the compass on which to fix his eyes, for so small was his circle of visibility that the steep seas came charging in from the fog at seemingly impossible angles, and there was no suggestion of a straight horizon line. Nevertheless we tried to keep some sort of a look-out, fearful that the morning's terrifying experience might be repeated, and that at any moment a ship might silently loom up bows on. We now kept a frequently refilled hot-water bottle in our communal bunk, but in spite of that, and though the watch below turned in fully clad, our teeth continued to chatter.

That night the wind took off, and in the early hours of the morning we lay becalmed with the sails slamming dreadfully in the left-over sea. Worn out by the excitements of the past twenty-four hours, we took down the headsail, hardened the mainsail right in, hung the riding light in the rigging, and putting our faith in God and the radar reflector—to hell with a look-out—both turned in and slept well.

And that was the end of what we call our 'Nantucket nightmare'. At dawn the sky cleared, and soon the rising sun gave just a hint of warmth to tempt Nicholson out of the dank cabin where the teak floor was dark with wet. Progress with a light, fair wind was slow, but what a relief it was to see a sharp, clear horizon after days of poor visibility, and that night Polaris, which we had last seen nine nights before, now hung high in the sky to tell of the northing we had made.

Soon after noon of our twelfth day at sea we sighted the hills of Mount Desert Island, and that evening we sailed gently in beside them towards Bar Harbor, pilotage being made easy by the many splendidly painted buoys. Our ears were filled with the cries of birds (among them many black-back gulls) and the roar of lobster boats' open exhausts, and our eyes with the green slopes of the lovely island, the hills of which are higher than any others on the east coast.

◀

24. The cobblestoned waterfront street of Mystic Seaport, reconstructed by the Marine Historical Association as a typical New England seaport community of the mid-nineteenth century.

That evening as we lay at anchor in a quiet cove near Bar Harbor we realized once again how full of contrasts cruising is. Not only had the anxiety and discomfort of the foggy passage been replaced by a feeling of complete relaxation and a sense almost of luxury, but since leaving the Bahamas the westerly magnetic variation had changed from 1 to 18 degrees; the mean air temperature had fallen from 80 to 45 degrees Fahrenheit, and the sea from 75 to 40; the sun now set much later, and instead of an onrush of night there was a long period of lingering twilight. Above all, we had exchanged the low, scrub-covered, limestone islands for the pink granite and dark green spruce trees of Maine.

7

MAINE TO CHESAPEAKE

'Do you think,' said Susan as she gave a final rub to the polished brass in the hatchway, 'that we shall have to wait much longer for the customs? I want to get ashore and buy some of that American steak we've heard so much about.'

'Well,' I said doubtfully, 'we've only had "Q" flying for an hour, and I wouldn't want to put a foot wrong in our first port. You remember what they told us about American officials when we were in the Bahamas; how they hate yachts, and make life difficult for them.'

'Yes, but that was in Florida. They may be different here.'

We waited another half-hour, but then as nobody had come off to us we launched the dinghy and rowed for the shore.

I like rowing ashore at the end of a passage, especially when it has been a rough or difficult one, and between glances over my shoulder I can have a good look at the little green and white ship that has brought us there. Susan usually shares this pleasure with me, as we are in the habit of sitting side by side on the centre thwart of the dinghy and taking an oar each, which is a good way of getting along provided we both have the same destination in mind; but I find I have to vary my stroke a bit now and then because when Susan sees something of particular interest she is inclined to stop rowing. How trim *Wanderer* looked, I thought, and how gay with the stars and stripes fluttering from her starboard crosstree above the yellow 'Q' flag, and the blue ensign streaming out from its gold-topped staff at the stern. I pictured her as she had been only such a short time before, rushing through the fog with streaming decks

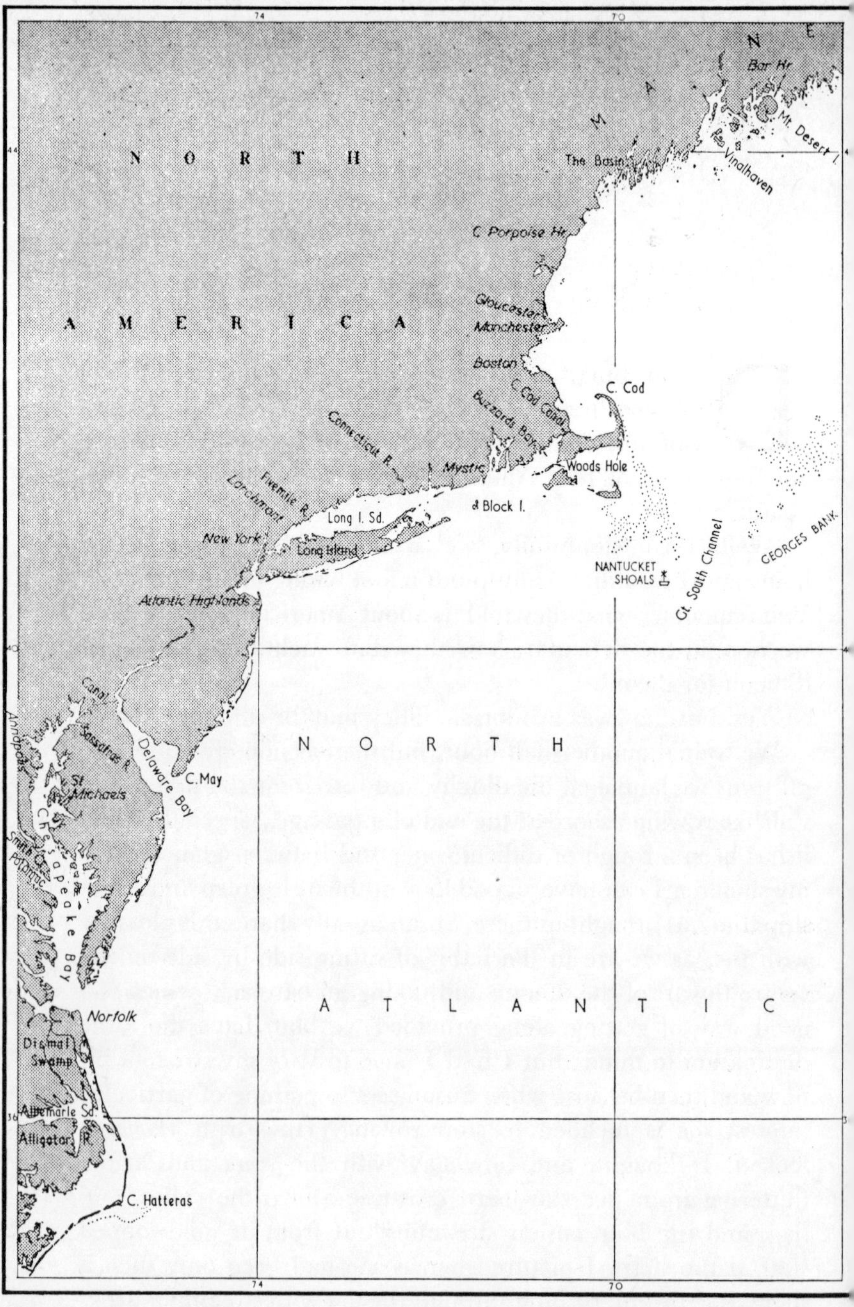

EAST COAST OF UNITED STATES

from Mount Desert Island to Cape Hatteras

and a high bow-wave, and I wished I could have been aboard the Nantucket lightvessel to see her make her sudden ghost-like appearance out of the fog, and then vanish as quickly as she had come. If anyone aboard did see her, they could never have known whence she came or whither bound. An enigma.

On the quay we found a tourist bureau. We had not expected this, for we did not then know that Maine is one of the country's vacationlands, and that all cars registered in the state have that word on their number plates. We told the pleasant woman behind the counter that we were off the little yacht out there, and had just come from the Bahamas. She seemed a bit uncertain about those far-off islands, but quickly understood our need.

'You want the customs, I think,'—and she picked up the telephone.

A few minutes later a car with two officers appeared.

'Welcome to Maine'—as they shook our hands. 'Let's head for the office right away.'

'But don't you want to go on board?' I asked, remembering how port officials in most parts of the world like to sit in the cabin while they ask questions, fill in forms, and have a drink. But apparently this was not necessary, and after a short drive along wide roads well shaded by trees all dressed in young green foliage, we reached the terminal where the car ferry from Yarmouth, Nova Scotia, berths, and were shown into a bright, clean office. Our hosts plied us with coffee and doughnuts while they took down some particulars and issued us with a cruising permit, which entitled us to take *Wanderer* anywhere we liked along the coast without further formality for a period of six months.

'But what do we do when it expires?' I asked. 'We expect to be in your country for a bit longer than that.'

The older man clapped me on the shoulder and said:

'You just go to the nearest custom house and ask for a new one. Just ask, that's all.'

So much for the stories of American official ogres, I thought, as they whisked us back to the town, where Susan was able to shop to her heart's content, and the tourist bureau told us where to go, what to see, and presented us with a handful of maps.

We were to find as the months sped by and we cruised west and south along the coast, that such friendly and efficient treatment was typical; the assistants in the shops, the clerks in the banks and post offices, nearly always did their best to help us and make our visit enjoyable, and so did the people in the higher-income brackets that we had the good fortune to meet. We were luckier than some visitors, for we even found the cab drivers friendly and ready to talk about their families or hobbies, but we did not put this to the test in New York. We sometimes wished that our experiences—putting in at many places, meeting some of the inhabitants, and learning a little about their way of life—could be shared by some of the people in Britain who, perhaps mistaking politics for real life, are so critical of America. We found that many of our acquaintances had a clear and sympathetic understanding of some of Britain's troubles, and were refreshingly modest about their own country's achievements, no matter whether these were the exploration of outer space or the winning of a yacht race. But our experiences were limited entirely to the east coast.

The yachtsman from Long Island Sound, where there is a great gathering of craft (45,000 in the eastern part alone, I believe), probably regards Maine in much the same light as the South Coast of England sailing man regards West Scotland, that is, a desirable though perhaps rugged cruising ground, reasonably easy of access, but not too easy to return from, because the summer wind along the New England coast usually blows from south-west, and is therefore a headwind for the homeward trip. Maine is a place of rivers and inlets, of inshore and offshore islands, and although parts of its coast are fringed by holiday homes, some of them with ten bedrooms, or more, there are many beautiful and unspoilt anchorages. This coast, with its cool, clean atmosphere, was our happy cruising ground for some weeks, during which we nosed our way into all manner of lovely coves, which might be anything between 5 and 25 miles apart, and some were so remote that we could sit on deck and listen to the silence, which was broken only by the ticking of the cabin clock and now and then by the cry of a bird or the splash of a jumping fish. But Maine, like Cape Cod, has a lot of fog in summer, and although we did not experience the 20 per cent to which we were entitled, we had enough of it to keep the navigator on his toes. Often when we awoke in the morning we found our still anchorage shrouded; usually the sun burnt through in the forenoon and the fog 'scaled up', but sometimes we lay all day in a small, silent world of our own, and enjoyed the novelty of it. However, there was little pleasure to be had when, a clear fine morning having tempted us out to make a passage to the next harbour, fog suddenly came rolling in on the breath of an onshore breeze to obscure everything; then we felt tense as we steered by compass, anxiously waiting for the next buoy to come into view, hoping meanwhile that the tidal stream was not setting us off our course. It came in 'kinda soupy' one day just as we were picking our way among the rocks, islands and tidal swirls which guard the eastern end of Eggemoggin Reach (one of many channels between the islands and the shore) and the best we could do was grope our way to an anchorage in the lee of a small, uninhabited island, guided by the cries of sea-birds on the beach, and wait there for it to lift. Incidentally, I noticed that people giving sailing directions for these waters, such as Blanchard in his excellent *Cruising Guide to the New England Coast*, never say 'In the event of fog . . .' or 'Should you have the misfortune to encounter fog . . .' or 'If it is foggy . . .' Instead they just say 'In the fog . . .', implying that this is the prevailing weather condition, and thereby striking fear into the heart of the stranger.

However, on this coast the high percentage of fog is not quite such a hazard as it might be elsewhere, as, for example, on the coasts of Britain, for there is a profusion of buoys (pronounced bu-oys), each one clearly painted and numbered, and distances between them are small. The U.S. Coastguard, which is responsible for buoys and lighthouses among many other things, does not subscribe to the lateral system of uniform buoyage, but has its own system. which we found clearer and easier to use. Entering an estuary, river, or harbour, red conical buoys called 'nuns' must be left to starboard, and black cans to port, and the easy way to remember this is 'red right returning' and 'black right out'. Black-and-red buoys mark middle grounds or isolated dangers. Usually a buoy at a turning or other important point has a gong or bell (a gong giving several notes, a bell only one) or a whistle. In addition there are many lighthouses with fog signals, and a fair supply of radio beacons. Woods Hole Passage is a good example of the thorough manner in which the Coastguard marks difficult places. This is not in Maine, but lies to the south-west of that state, and is between the Cape Cod peninsula and the Elizabeth Islands. Including its approaches, the passage is only 2¼ miles long, yet it is marked by four lighthouses, four beacons, and twenty-one buoys, of which seven are lighted and several have radar reflectors. For a stranger so many aids can cause confusion, and it is essential to have up-to-date American charts. I enjoyed using these charts, which are comparatively cheap yet are clear and detailed, but I never quite felt at home with the datum to which they are reduced, which is that of mean low water, instead of low water springs, for the actual water-level can drop several feet below that datum.

Apart from the fog (I see I have got into the habit now!), the weather during our time in Maine was fine; indeed, it was sometimes almost too fine, and I believe our engine there used more fuel than its predecessor had used on an entire circumnavigation of the world, as day followed day of almost complete calm; but we did have one or two jolly little sails when the sea sparkled and the spray flew. We saw few other yachts, for it was still a little early in the season.

We have many happy memories of Maine. In Vinalhaven Island, for example, having threaded our way through some narrow, crooked channels, we came to Long Cove, secured to one of several moorings there, and had the place entirely to ourselves. The float of the mooring, like most others in those ▶

25. The full-rigged ship *Joseph Conrad*, which Alan Villiers sailed round the world, seen in the early-morning calm at Mystic over the bows of the Chesapeake oyster dredger *Dorothy A. Parsons*.

DOROTHY A. PARSONS.

parts, was a 5-foot-long log of wood shackled direct to the riding chain, and with a hole at its upper end for the user to reeve a line through; the reason for this is that the majority of the harbours freeze over during the winter, and the normal type of buoy on a rope would almost certainly get cut adrift. Close by was a cat-size island—a smooth, granite rock with some small trees growing in a crevice on its summit—the perfect playground for Nicholson; not so large that he could get lost, not so small that there was much risk of him falling off it in a moment of inattention. The mooring, the island, and most of the west side of this beautiful, long and narrow inlet, belonged to Richard Pratt, a member of the Cruising Club of America. Soon after our arrival in Maine he had persuaded the coastguards to find us (which they did by high-speed launch) and deliver a message inviting us to make use of his property. He was not there, but he heard of our visit and has since changed the island's name to Cat-Size Island.

One of the introductions given to us by Bob Rimington was to Sandy Moffat, probably the greatest living authority on cruising in Maine. We had had some correspondence with him and now were invited to his summer home at Crockett's Cove, only 2 miles away, to attend his seventy-fifth birthday party; he arrived by yacht precisely at the appointed hour, which was no mean feat, as he had come a considerable distance in the fog. It was some party. The house was full of Moffats, dozens of them, it seemed, and Susan and I became thoroughly confused, owing to two brothers having married two sisters.

Another unforgettable occasion, though of a different kind, was the day we spent in The Basin up the New Meadows river in fog so thick that we could scarcely see the near-by shore, on which we landed to walk silently on a soft carpet of pine needles under the dripping trees, and listened to the tolling of some distant bell buoy.

Now that the timber mills and stone quarries are little

◀

26. The last surviving wooden whaling ship, *Charles W. Morgan*, with the slender whaleboats from which 2,500 whales were harpooned and killed, has found her last resting-place at Mystic after an active life of eighty years.

worked, and the cutting and storing of pond ice has been abandoned, the chief coastal industries in Maine are looking after the holidaymakers and their houses, and fishing for lobsters, which is done by a hardy bunch of individualists. At Cape Porpoise Harbor we were fortunate enough to be invited by one of these men to his home to meet his wife and his mother-in-law. The former was cooking lunch in the living-room-kitchen in which we all sat; there were two huge refrigerators as well as the stove, and the walls and shelves were remarkably filled with bric-à-brac. His mother-in-law sat in a rocking-chair making nets of nylon string for the home-made lobster traps. While we ate hamburgers and drank coffee we learnt a little about a lobsterman's business. Often he builds his own lean and swift transom-stern 30-footer, and provides her with a wheelhouse, the port or starboard side of which is left open, depending on whether he works his traps left- or right-handed, and the mizen mast with its little steadying sail is placed on the opposite side. He powers her with some old car or truck engine picked up for a few dollars on the scrap-heap, couples up a belt-driven winch to haul his lines, and as he fits no silencer, he can be heard for miles. He works all the year round, usually single-handed, and in the winter has to follow the lobster a long way offshore to get his catch. Fog does not appear to bother him much, but he dreads snow. All up and down the coast, and even in the harbours, the lobster-trap floats, usually brightly painted plastic bottles, lie so thick and close together that it is hazardous to try to pass between them under power; at Cape Porpoise they say that at the height of the season you can walk across the harbour on them—if you are wearing snowshoes.

We had, as I say, very little wind in Maine; we had even less along the New Hampshire coast, and off Massachusetts none at all except during the evening when we were approaching Gloucester. This is the port from which many of the Banks fishing schooners used to sail, and was immortalized by Rudyard Kipling in *Captains Courageous*, and by Longfellow, who wrecked the schooner *Hesperus* there on the Reef of Norman's Woe. Off near-by Cape Ann we picked up the first real wind we had encountered in weeks, and were soon scudding towards the harbour, pursued by a great bank of blue-black cloud. We had just rounded the outer breakwater when down came the rain in torrents just after a jagged fork of lightning had ripped across the sky, and all was hidden from us. By compass we steered for a buoy marking a shoal (not Norman's Woe, I am glad to say) and made small circles round it until the rain let up and the wind moderated, enabling us to find our way in to the inner harbour, where we tied up alongside a motor yacht for the night, as the place was too crowded to permit us to anchor.

Soon after our arrival in America we had received a gift of all the necessary large-scale charts from the Boston Station of the Cruising Club of America, together with an invitation from Bill Brewer, Rear Commodore of that Station, to visit Manchester, where he lived. So we headed there from Gloucester, and found a beautiful, countrified inlet accommodating 500 fine yachts, and at its head a pleasing little town. We were boarded at the yacht club and piloted to a snug mooring right off Bill Brewer's house, where he and his wife Ann made us welcome, put their guest house with its hot-water supply at our disposal, and gave us such a splendid time that we stayed for a week and enjoyed every moment of it. We felt at home there, we felt settled and relaxed, and it was hard to tear ourselves away.

Fifty miles on we came to the deep-water canal which cuts through the isthmus joining the great hook of Cape Cod (outside which we had passed on our passage north) to the rest of Massachusetts, and anchored for a night in the clean and comfortable basin at its east end. Including the approach channel, the canal is just over 10 miles long, and like other American canals we subsequently used, is free of tolls. There are no locks, and because of the difference in range of tide and times of high water at its ends, the tidal streams run strongly through it and can attain a rate of 5 knots. We wished to take the morning's west-going stream through the canal, but when we got outside the basin at dawn we found the traffic signal against us. We returned to our anchorage for an hour and then tried again, but still the light was red, and by the time we had learnt from the Corps of Engineers' office ashore that yachts should disregard the signals, the fair stream had finished. So we had to make our transit on the afternoon tide, though this was something we had wanted to avoid because of the chance of encountering a headwind at the far (Buzzards Bay) end. And sure enough the usual afternoon south-wester was blowing fresh by the time we had passed under the last lift bridge, and against the tide it raised so steep a little sea that our motor could make no headway against it, so, there being no other traffic about, we made sail and beat out.

In the Buzzards Bay–Cape Cod area we visited many of the pleasant harbours with which the area abounds, and found some of them overfilled with yachts; but there was plenty of room at windy Block Island, where a large freshwater lake had been opened up as a harbour by the simple but expensive method of digging a channel from it to the sea, and rigging it up with buoys and leading lights. This is typical of the kind of thing that is done by the state for yachting, which is regarded not only as an important sport but as big business.

Surely no visitor to these waters would miss the opportunity of taking his vessel up the Mystic river on the Connecticut shore, to lie alongside at Mystic Seaport, the Marine Historical Association's museum, where some of the most interesting exhibits lie afloat. But when I telephoned the dockmaster from Block Island he said there would be no berth available for several days. So we went instead to near-by Stonington, intending to travel in from there by bus or taxi, but Duke Winter, the manager of a Stonington boatyard, took pity on us when he saw us standing forlornly in the empty street, invited us into his car and drove us to Mystic, where the Director of the Seaport, Waldo Johnson, gave us lunch and assured us that a berth for *Wanderer* was available and, indeed, had been reserved for her ever since he had heard she was in the area. We therefore ▶

27. *Left:* Manhattan by night from my lofty hotel bedroom and, *right,* from the top of the Empire State Building. Both were splendid views, but to us not so exciting as . . .

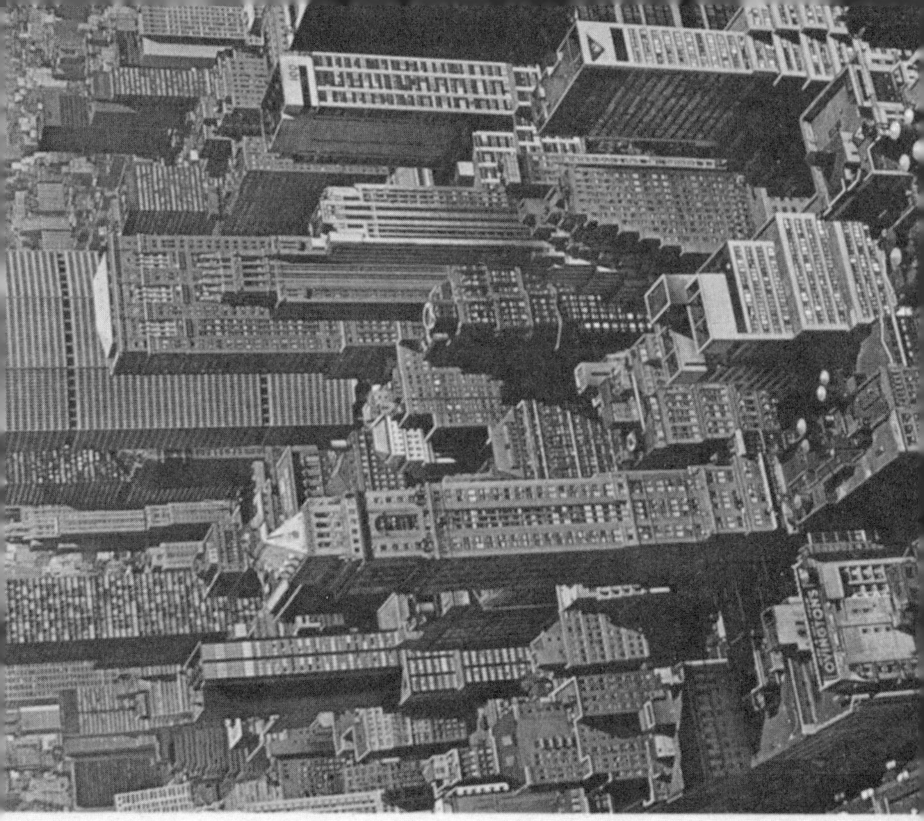

returned to Stonington, and with Duke as pilot, sailed *Wanderer* round and up the river, and as we passed through the second of the opening bridges and the masts and yards of the old ships lying at the Seaport came into view, we noticed that since our morning visit all of them had been dressed over all with flags. After an embarrassing exhibition before a large audience of how not to turn round in a tideway, we brought *Wanderer* alongside beneath the great flagpole where the Union flag was immediately broken out in her honour. We were astonished and much moved by this quite unexpected welcome. Although we remained as guests for three days, we did not see as much of the exhibits as we would have liked, for not only were we entertained very generously, but we spent a lot of time answering questions, just as we had at Boat Shows in the past, for many of the 5,000 daily visitors seemed to think that *Wanderer* was one of the floating exhibits, and they were particularly interested in her vane gear, such as is not often to be found aboard American yachts.

However, early each morning we had the fascinating place almost to ourselves, and then were able to stroll along the cobbled, quayside street with its ropewalk and sail-loft, apothecary shop, shipsmith shop, cooperage, and counting house, and stand and stare, and dream of the hard but rewarding seafaring days of the last century. Often we paused beside the only surviving wooden whaling ship, the *Charles W. Morgan*, to look up at the slender white boats, from which some 2,500 whales had been harpooned, and above them at the lofty masts and widespread yards. In an eventful and profitable working life of eighty years, this ship made thirty-seven voyages, some of them extending for three years, and the master often took his wife along to share the gimballed bed in his tiny cabin. Every corner of the ship was redolent of whale oil. Sometimes we stopped on the quay underneath the long bowsprit of the Banks fishing schooner *L. A. Dunton*, which overhung it, tracing her rigging

◄

28. . . . seeing the skyscraper skyline from the deck of our own small ship as she hurried with the tide down the East River.

against the sky, and noting how neatly her dories nested on deck. On one occasion I was escorted up to the foretop of the ship *Joseph Conrad*, which Alan Villiers sailed round the world and took into the dangerous waters of the Coral Sea, by an attractive but silent young woman who had a summer job at the Seaport. I was dismayed to find that the top was not provided with the usual lubber's hole, and that I had instead to go out over the futtock shrouds like a proper sailor; at the moment of hanging by my hands with the planking of the deck a long, long way below, the movie camera which was slung over my shoulder suddenly felt unbearably heavy.

We were a little apprehensive about cruising through the 100 miles of Long Island Sound towards New York, for where else in the world could one find pleasure craft in such vast numbers? Apart from the Connecticut river—where there is plenty of room for sailing and many uncluttered anchorages, such as that in Selden Creek, which is so narrow that we had difficulty in turning round in it—all the sheltered harbours would be so full of yachts that a berth for us might not be available, while at the back of our minds lay the nagging thought that August is a bad month for hurricanes, and that these sometimes make their way north along the coast instead of heading out to sea; so we might need a hurricane cellar one day.

However, helpful people we met along the way always seemed able and willing to pass us on to a club or a friend ahead, with the result that wherever we needed a mooring for a night or for several nights one was available for us. Most yacht clubs have accommodation for the transient visitor, either a guest mooring or a berth alongside a pier, and if the former, the club boatman on hearing three blasts of one's foghorn will come out to ferry one ashore.

Two things much impressed us apart from the great number of yachts: the cleanliness of the water—we rarely saw a slick of oil or any floating rubbish, for it is an offence to throw anything over the side—and the good-mannered seamanship of the boat-owners. But we did learn that it is not wise to try to sail in Long

Island Sound in light winds during the week-end, for the confusion of wakes from the many power craft, most of which appeared to have an excess of power capable of driving them far beyond their proper hull speed, bounced us about so much that at times we could make no progress. We hit bottom only once, but hard and on rock, while leaving the anchorage at Hay Island. This should not have happened, as the place is not particularly difficult, and probably would not have happened had it not been for some sticks standing vertically in the water; mistakenly we supposed that these marked dangers, instead of being connected, as perhaps we should have guessed, with some form of fishing. But along the east coast the Americans permit their fishermen all sorts of liberties and allow them to lay booby traps for the unwary in a pretty big way. I have already mentioned the inconvenience of the thousands of lobster-trap floats, which could be a danger to a power-driven vessel at night; but, worse than this, hundreds of square miles of navigable waters are neatly ruled off on the charts by dashed magenta lines, and a note explains that these are fish-trap areas; the traps one can see in daylight and avoid, though not easily by night; but, horrors! the note on the chart states also that submerged piling may exist within these areas. Considering how much is done by the state for the comfort, convenience, and safety of yachts, it astonished us that this last danger, benefiting so few, is allowed to persist.

After twenty years of correspondence, Bob Rimington, of *Yachting*, and I met at last. This was at his week-end retreat near Fivemile River, where he and his wife Jay were most kind to us and gave us the opportunity to meet some other interesting people. One of these was Bob Bavier, America's Cup helmsman, and a more modest or interesting sailing man it would be hard to find; unlike some other racing skippers I have met, he claimed that his success was due entirely to his crew, and he seemed to have a high regard for Peter Scott, who had skippered the last challenging British 12-metre. We also met Fred Adams, at that time Commodore of the Cruising Club of America, and his wife; they had recently returned from a troublesome transatlantic race in which they had lost their mizen mast and seriously bent the main mast (both were of alloy), but managed to effect repairs and continue on their way. Knowing that we were in need of boards to place between our fenders and piles when lying alongside, and a copy of a book on the Chesapeake, they drove us to their home after the Rimington party and gave us both.

It was from the yachting port of Larchmont that Susan and I commuted by rail to New York on several days to see the sights and attend to some business. My publisher's New York office had arranged for me to take part in a television parlour game called *To Tell the Truth*, and this entailed spending a night at the Americana Hotel, where I had a splendid view of the city by night from my lofty bedroom window. To play *To Tell the Truth* three people claimed to be Eric Hiscock, two impostors and myself, and a highly coloured précis of my cruising exploits was read. We faced a panel of four television personalities, and each of them asked each of us questions in turn for a short time. The impostors were allowed to give any answers they liked to mislead and endeavour to prove they were the real E.H., but I had to answer always with the truth, though I could be as hesitant as I wished. At the end each member of the panel decided which of us was the real E.H., and for every wrong guess we three got $100 to split between us. That did not seem to me to be very generous payment for a show which is said to be viewed by twelve million people, but to me the most interesting part was finding out what sort of people C.B.S. had roped in to impersonate me. Both, of course, had been selected because they spoke with English accents; the rotund red-faced one said he was a retired brigadier now working as a consulting engineer, and soon after we met he tried to sell me for $20 an old telescope which he suddenly produced mysteriously. The tall, tough- ▶

29. While cruising on the east coast of America we passed 151 bridges, most of which had to open to let us through, but here are two of the fixed ones. *Top:* The Verrazano suspension bridge, which makes a ¾-mile leap between Long and Staten islands just south of New York. *Bottom:* A high bridge over the Delaware and Chesapeake canal, photographed from up *Wanderer*'s mast while she lay at anchor in the canal basin near Chesapeake City.

looking one with high-peaked eyebrows and a black moustache wore bracelets of elephant hair, one of which he gave to me; he claimed to be a white hunter, and to prove it he handed round during rehearsal, and much to the dismay of the producer, a set of photographs showing a pair of lions copulating, and he explained that this continued at twenty-minute intervals for four and a half days.

Only one of the panel, a man, voted for me as the real Eric Hiscock, and when the compère asked him why, he replied:

'Well, he looks old and frail and pale' (no doubt I did beside my massive and colourful companions) 'and it is usually people like that who go off and do crazy things such as sailing round the world.'

To say that we found Manhattan clean, courteous, quiet (traffic-wise), and in parts, such as the Rockefeller Center, excitingly beautiful, is no exaggeration; but we made the mistake of going up the Empire State Building on a Wednesday, when 34,998 other people decided to use the elevators, and queueing for the trip both up and down took the better part of two hours. The view, of course, was splendid, but to us not so exciting as seeing the fantastic skyscraper skyline of Manhattan from the deck of our own small ship, as she hurried with the tide down the busy East River and under the eight great bridges that span it. From Larchmont we made our way down past the thin green marvel of the United Nations building, like a huge glass tray standing on end beside the river, and out past the Battery and the Statue of Liberty, where shipping from all four corners of the world converged, their wakes crossed by interweaving ferry boats and tugs. On we went through the Narrows, where the span of the Verrazano bridge makes its spectacular ¾-mile leap between Long and Staten Islands, dwarfing our tiny vessel as she slipped through its shadow. In the afternoon of that exciting day, and having carried a fair tide all the way from Larchmont—this was just as well, as we knew of no good

◀

30. Like a raddled actress awaiting her cue in the wings of some great theatre, *Wanderer* spends the night in a floodlit travelift up the Sassafras river.

intermediate stopover in that 40-mile stretch—we came to an anchorage in Atlantic Highlands artificial harbour inside Sandy Hook.

After a night's rest we rounded the Hook, and in poor visibility headed along the New Jersey coast, and the day being a Sunday, threaded our way among many craft all packed with amateur fishermen, their rods projecting like pins from a pincushion, and after a night passage (the only one in all our time on the American coast) just managed to beat the fog in a neck-and-neck race to Cape May harbour.

In that rather dreary place we were 'buzzed' so mercilessly by youths in speed-boats with open exhausts that we took refuge in the excellent Cold Spring marina, which has berths for about 200 yachts. There we remained for several days, because each morning there was fog, and we wished to make an early start so as to have daylight for the trip through Cape May canal, up Delaware Bay, and through another canal to the head of Chesapeake Bay, a total distance of 64 miles without a safe or convenient stopping-place along the way. Our first attempt came to nothing, for no sooner had we passed through the Cape May canal and got fairly out into the Delaware than the north-west wind, for which we had hoped in vain ever since we reached Maine, put in an appearance, and we quickly learnt why that stretch of shallow, discoloured water has such a bad reputation. Unable to make reasonable headway against the short, steep sea, and knowing of no other place we could reach in daylight (the Delaware is no place to play about in after dark, with its stream of big ships in the narrow fairway, and its fish stakes elsewhere), we returned to our comfortable marina for another night. This cost $3.50, but with our own floating pontoon and water supply with which to wash off the crust of salt, hot showers, and the friendly company of other boating people—some apparently berthed permanently there because of their need for mains electricity—we did not consider that unreasonable.

Next day we again made an early start. In a calm we once more motored through the canal, which by now we thought might be getting tired of stopping traffic and opening bridges for us, but at the far end we picked up a fine beam wind. Under full sail *Wanderer* hurried along to such purpose that she averaged $6\frac{1}{2}$ knots all the way from the marina at Cape May to Chesapeake City; but she did have a good push from the tide, for the farther north you go in the Delaware the later does the stream turn against you, and by sailing fast that day we actually had a fair stream for the entire 64-mile trip. (This must be an awkward place for small craft trying to go in the opposite direction.)

Like the Cape Cod canal, the 15-mile-long Chesapeake and Delaware canal has no locks, and again because of the tidal differences at its ends, the stream flows through it with some strength. Fortunately, as I have said, we had it with us, for under power we could never have made headway against it and the fresh wind, which was ahead as soon as we entered the canal. We made our number with the Corps of Engineers' tug at the entrance, giving our height of mast, which she radioed to the bridge-tenders ahead; the lifting span of the first great bridge close by rose courteously a few feet higher than we needed, and making only about 2 knots through the water, we motored majestically under. We met some tugs pushing trains of lighters, and some fast motor yachts, which made a great commotion with their steep wakes, but little else in that usually busy commercial waterway. In several places work was in progress widening the canal, much of which lies between barren, artificial banks, which are too high to permit a view of the low countryside beyond. We found a new short cut for which our chart had not prepared us, and across it another lift bridge, a railroad one this time; but unlike the other it lifted only enough to permit our burgee stick to pass with a bare few inches to spare. Most yachts passing through, unlike ourselves (To Tell the Truth!) exaggerate their mast heights so as to allow a margin of safety, and perhaps that bridge-tender was aware of this and had taken to using his own fine judgement. By sundown we were at anchor in the comfortable basin opposite Chesapeake City, which is little more than a village.

Wanderer had not been out of the water since she went on the slip at Martinique nine months before, and during that time we had kept her bottom clean by diving; but we had long ago scrubbed off most of the antifouling paint, and were finding that the oxidized copper sheathing was tending to become foul more and more quickly. As Chesapeake Bay is not a good place for swimming because of the large number of sea nettles (poisonous jelly-fish), we made our way as soon as we had left the canal up the winding Sassafras river to a big yacht yard, and there arranged to be lifted out on a travelift, a type of mobile crane on rails. The yard manager, knowing how hard pressed we must be for dollars, kindly allowed us to do our own work—this is contrary to the general rule—and even lent us paint-brushes. With the slings of the travelift still round her, *Wanderer* spent the night on the concrete apron, her green and white sides and her red underwater body splendidly bathed in the beams from four great floodlights—a raddled actress awaiting her cue in the wings of some great theatre.

But unfortunately a mishap occurred while she was being lowered into the water next morning: unnoticed by any of us, some part of the lift—this was not designed for handling vessels with tall masts—fouled one of her upper crosstrees and wrenched it off. To remove the broken fitting for welding, the mast had to come out, and as the yard had no men accustomed to rigging, Susan and I did most of the work ourselves.

We had other troubles to contend with that day. From an accumulation of mail which had just reached us, we learnt that our tenants at home had not been paying any rent for some time, nor were they likely to do in the forseeable future, and that the County Council was seizing some of our land for road-widening purposes. Charts we had ordered and paid for had not arrived, but a set of batteries for the tape-recorder had, and the price had risen 300 per cent. While tuning in to get a weather forecast the belt drive of the radio set started to slip, and when I came to write up my daily journal I found that my fountain pen, which is one of the sort that is supposed to fill itself by capillary attraction, refused to drink a drop of ink. The final disaster, which with a wife less equable than Susan could have caused a domestic crisis, occurred after I had cleaned out a paint-brush on a paper bag and put this in the garbage bucket; Susan, wishing to dispose of a piece of bad meat, picked up the bag and got her hands covered with green paint. Clearly this was not our day.

However, the yard manager treated us generously and well; he declined to accept any payment for lifting or for the gallon of expensive antifouling paint we had used, and he docked us free and gave us the run of the place for several days. By mid-September, with a clean bottom and everything shipshape aloft, we were ready to explore a little of Chesapeake Bay on our way south.

This is the largest body of inland water on the Atlantic coast of the U.S.A., being about 170 miles long and from 3 to 23 miles wide. Into it flow nearly forty rivers, all of which have smaller rivers and creeks flowing into them, and tucked away in little coves and bends of these creeks lie countless snug and land-locked anchorages, many of them out of sight and sound of man and all his works except for farming; one could spend years cruising there and then not know a half of them. But just in case the pleasure of finding one's way under sail into, and stopping at these beautiful, silent berths among the farmlands should pall after a time, on the shores of the many-armed bay, which has been likened to 'the deck plan of an octopus', stand several towns, both large and small, waiting to be explored, and there are a lot of friendly and charming people to be met. The charts are excellent, the buoyage adequate, and although in some places, particularly along the Eastern Shore, 'the water's spread kinda thin', pilotage did not present us with many problems, though once or twice we were almost led astray by the shape of a beacon's topmark; what should have been a triangle appeared to be a rectangle because, as we found on a closer approach, some bird had built a huge nest on it; also we sometimes had to go many miles out of our way to avoid fish-trap areas such as I have mentioned earlier. A particular attraction is that because of the small range of tide, sometimes no more than a few inches, the creeks give the impression of enjoying permanent high water, with trees and grass growing right down to the water's edge, and no mud showing.

We cruised the Chesapeake in the autumn, which is considered to be one of the best times of year, because the thunderstorms with their violent winds, which are frequent in summer, have finished, and insects are less troublesome, though we were at times glad of our mosquito screens. But this, of course, is the hurricane season; indeed, during our visit Inez, the ninth that year, went on the rampage down among the West Indies, where her winds of 170 knots did much damage and killed 200 people before she headed for Florida and lost intensity, leaving the West Indies to Judith, her successor. But fortunately hurricanes rarely enter the Chesapeake.

The first town we called at was Annapolis, which for a short time nearly 200 years ago was the nation's capital. The yacht club gave us a berth alongside free of charge, and the reporter who came to get our story, a kindly woman who had at one time been on the stage, drove us round to see the sights, including the fine old State House in which George Washington resigned his commission, and the vast Naval Academy. Another town we called at was St. Michael's; this is on the Eastern Shore, which we considered the best side of the bay, because it is more isolated in spite of the two great bridges which link it to the Western Shore, and has fewer visitors, while its people live a quieter, more rural life. Unlike the usual American town, which is widely spread and demands some form of transport, St. Michaels is small and compact and easy to shop in on foot, its old timber houses looking out between the trees at one another across the red brick, herringbone-pattern sidewalks.

On the way to it we put in for a day or two at charming Tilghman Creek, where we were hailed by two elderly men in a small sloop asking if they might come alongside us and have a 'gam'. These were 'the Fowler boys', Francis and Fred, twins aged 79, amusing companions and great experts on cruising in those waters. After they had been talking with us in our cabin for a time, Susan noticed that Nicholson was absent, and on going on deck to look for him discovered that he had boarded the Fowlers' yacht, found their roll of toilet tissue, and brought it into our cockpit, where with tooth and claw he was silently ripping it to shreds. Fortunately our visitors were amused by this prank. 'That'll be something to put in the log,' they chuckled, and they must have spread the story ahead of us, because, on arrival at St. Michaels, we found ourselves, or at least Nicholson, not entirely unknown, and were at once invited by Dundas Leavitt to berth at the Chesapeake Bay Maritime Museum, of which he was the Chairman, where he gave us a neat little dock to ourselves and the free run of the place.

The museum is devoted entirely to the history of the bay and its ships, and like its big sister at Mystic has some floating exhibits. At the time of our visit Dundas was arranging for the transport, all in one piece, of the now disused lighthouse and dwelling from Hooper's Strait to the museum, but busy though he must have been he gave up an entire afternoon to showing us around. This was the beginning of a friendship we value highly, and when he invited us to share with his trimaran the dock beside his home at Bailey's Neck on the Tred Avon river, we jumped at the opportunity, and we spent a happy time there with him and his wife. He arranged for the generous owner/pilot of a charter plane to take us for a flight over the bay, and he gave us much of his wide knowledge of the Intracoastal Waterway, which soon we would be passing through. In early October, while we were still on the Eastern Shore, the great annual migration of geese was starting; the birds in their close-packed hundreds were coming in from the north to feed and rest, and many to remain in the sanctuaries, their thrilling honking filling the still air.

In Chesapeake Bay are to be found the only surviving commercial sailing vessels in American waters, a fleet of about fifty skipjacks, flat-bottom sloops with gingerbread-decorated clipper bows, broad sterns, and steeply raking masts. The chief business of the skipjack is dredging for oysters, and until recently under Maryland law she was permitted to do this only under sail, and police boats and helicopters patrol the bay to see the law enforced. But now the law has been modified to the extent that on Mondays and Tuesdays a skipjack may use her yawlboat—a motorized tender carried in davits over the stern—to nudge her across the oyster-beds. But crews are becoming difficult to find for this tough and poorly rewarded business, and a blight which kills the oysters is slowly creeping up the bay, so each year the fleet grows smaller.

Today it is common for British yacht clubs to organize meets (or rallies) for which members afloat gather in some selected harbour for a night or a week-end. The Cruising Club of America also has such meets, but often extends them over a week or more, and runs them in the form of a cruise in company, the fleet putting in at a different anchorage each day. *Wanderer* had been invited as guest ship to one of these cruises in the Chesapeake, but as the direction of the cruise did not coincide with her intended course, she was able to rendezvous only once with the fleet, and this she did at Smith Creek on the Potomac river. Twenty fine yachts arrived, and as is the American custom, rafted up, that is, lay alongside one another at anchor, and aboard them we found several old friends including the Brewers, who had been so good to us at Manchester, and Hank du Pont, who some years before had flown all the way to London to give Susan and me his club's Blue Water Medal. Continuous heavy rain did nothing to damp this jolly occasion (Americans seem to have a wonderful capacity for enjoyment), but we did find it difficult to recognize people wearing oilskin suits with hoods. During the night a strong wind caused the yachts forming some of the rafts to disperse, and in the morning all set sail, they to cross to the eastern shore, and we to head by way of several more attractive anchorages towards Norfolk, Virginia, down near the mouth of the bay.

▶

31. Annapolis, which stands on the Western Shore of the Chesapeake, was for a short time about 200 years ago the nation's capital. *Left:* The Governor's residence, and *right*, the dome of the State House in which George Washington resigned his commission.

8

THE INLAND WATERWAY

On the blue part of some maps of the east coast of the U.S.A. a red line can be seen leaving the port of Boston in the State of Massachusetts. This runs south to the Cape Cod canal, makes its way through Long Island Sound and New York harbour, gets almost lost in the shallow waterways of New Jersey, and after threading the Cape May canal emerges into Delaware bay. Up this it goes, passes through the canal into the Chesapeake, and having run down the middle of that great bay, plunges inland at Norfolk and never again ventures out into the open sea. This is the Intracoastal Waterway, and *Wanderer* had been on or close to it for most of its length so far, though she could not use the New Jersey part because it is too shallow and its bridges too low; but from now on she would follow it exactly for a thousand miles down almost to the tip of Florida, making her way through that part of it which is generally referred to as the Inland Waterway. This unique section consists of rivers, creeks, lakes, and estuaries, deepened where necessary by dredging, and connected one to another by artificial canals or 'cuts'.

We had in advance obtained the set of ten Waterway charts, each of which is 5 feet long, and usually shows two strips of the Waterway on each of its sides, but for convenient use is folded concertina fashion. These charts are drawn to a scale of about

◀

32. *Top:* Some of the charming old buildings which house the treasures of the Chesapeake Bay Maritime Museum at St. Michaels on the Eastern Shore. *Bottom:* Bailey's Neck, typical Chesapeake country, photographed from the air; *Wanderer* and Dundas Leavitt's trimaran share the dock beside his property. Boats without masts are often berthed under cover in little houses at the end of docks, as may be seen here.

2 inches to the nautical mile, and they give all necessary information: depths (the project depth is 10 to 12 feet, but many parts are shallower, and a vessel drawing more than 6 feet may experience difficulty in places); types of opening bridges, and the height of the few that do not open; all marinas are listed with their facilities and their distances from Norfolk, and tidal and radio information is given. The only inconvenience we found when using these charts was that because of the twisting nature of the Waterway, north is rarely at the top of a chart.

We had been studying these charts for some time, and had reached the conclusion that it would be necessary to make the greater part of the trip under power; this caused us some misgiving, for although *Wanderer* is an excellent and good-mannered little vessel under sail, she is not too easily manoeuvred under her low-powered motor and small propeller, especially in fresh winds. We were also concerned at the large number of bridges we would have to negotiate, and were worried by the stories we had heard of frequent strandings and calls to the Coastguard for assistance. We therefore felt a little apprehensive when, having dismantled and stowed below the vane steering gear, we set off one grey and windy day toward the end of October to find out for ourselves what the Waterway trip is really like.

The might of the U.S. Navy, rows of grey ships, some in commission, some fitting out, and many in mothballs, lay on either side as we motored up the river. Also there were colliers, tankers, and ore-carriers, and the air was acrid with the smoke from manufacturing plants. By the time we reached the fork where there is a choice of routes, five great bridges had without hesitation lifted or opened their steel spans to let us through, and we began to feel a little more confident. At the fork we turned to starboard so as to take the Dismal Swamp route instead of the deeper and faster alternative, for how could we resist investigating an area with such a strange name. This is the only part of the Waterway where there are any locks, one up and one down, and we had left the industry of the town well astern before reaching the first one at Deep Creek. Above it, as it was then evening, we tied up to the bank close to a 'carry-out' restaurant, from which we obtained a piping hot meal complete with everything, even disposable plates and forks. The motor yacht *Chinook*, in which Jim and Liz Emmett live and cruise, lay just ahead of us. I had corresponded with Jim about the Waterway, on which he is an expert, and it was fortunate for us that we fell in with him so early on our way, for he gave us a lot of information which we could not have obtained elsewhere.

The Dismal Swamp canal, surveyed by George Washington and dug by negro slaves, runs, with only one bend in its middle, straight and narrow for 20 miles, a mirror strip reflecting the sky between the trees growing in the swamp. Many of the trees, particularly the maples, were in full autumn dress, yellow, brown, red, and purple, and a strong wind bending their heads scattered the leaves like confetti on the coffee-coloured water, which lay so sheltered that the only ripples on it were those *Wanderer* made at her 4-knot gait. Far from being dismal, this was one of the loveliest sights we had seen for many a day. But when we brought up that evening in the old disused piece of canal at South Mills, which is so narrow that we had to moor the ship with anchors laid out ahead and astern to prevent her from swinging into the bank, and night, uncannily silent, set in, and the black trees seemed to crowd in more closely, we began to understand how the legends of ghosts and fugitives, of wild animals and poisonous snakes, and quicksands, had grown up. Also we had a fuller appreciation of the ballad entitled *The Lake of the Dismal Swamp*, which concerns a madman who wandered off into the swamp jungle in search of his love, and never returned:

> At the hour of midnight damp
> To cross the lake by a firefly lamp,
> And paddle their white canoe.

A few miles beyond that eerie anchorage the canal brought us to a river, winding and widening down to Elizabeth City, the last place where fuel and provisions can be had for the next 70 miles. This is one of the longest stretches without facilities on the Waterway, and it can be the most rugged, for it leads across

Albemarle Sound, which is so large that land cannot be seen in some directions, and in it a fresh wind can raise an awkward sea for small craft. We had hoped to sail across it and up the wide Alligator river, but there was so little wind that to avoid being benighted we kept the motor running nearly all the way, and in the evening entered another stretch of canal off which Dundas Leavitt had indicated a possible anchorage. On arrival there we nosed gently in, but grounded on something hard, probably a waterlogged tree-trunk; however, by keeping the motor running astern while we both went forward and swayed from side to side, we soon got off and continued along the canal to Fairfield swing bridge, where we found a disused cross-canal with a tiny dock at which a deserted power yacht was lying. The bridge tender suggested we lie alongside her, and presently her crew returned in a bad humour, for, it appeared, they were doing a delivery job and had miscalculated either the distance or their motor's consumption and had run out of fuel—we could imagine the owner's steaks from New York going bad in the now no longer cold deep-freeze. Knowing that Nicholson would not be able to resist going ashore across our neighbour, Susan asked a svelte blonde in the deckhouse if she minded cats.

'Ask the captain,' she replied without looking up from the paperback she was reading.

So Susan asked the captain.

'You'll have to keep it tied up,' was his reply.

Once before we had tried to keep Nicholson on board for a night, and he, being a great hunter, protested so much that neither of us got any sleep; so we cast off and moored with anchors fore-and-aft, and in the morning the power yacht, having somehow obtained some fuel, left and we took her berth.

This was a pleasant spot from which we could watch the Waterway traffic passing without being disturbed by its wash.

▶

33. The Inland Waterway runs through some of the wildest and least-known parts of the United States. *Top:* A mirror strip straight and narrow between the autumn-tinted trees, the Dismal Swamp canal, which was dug by slave labour, is the oldest in the country. *Bottom:* Susan explores an offshoot creek near Bucksport by dinghy.

Apart from yachts, the traffic mostly consists of blunt-bow tugs pushing one or more large barges; they are so skilfully handled that they do not constitute a hazard to other craft in daylight, but the powerful searchlights they use at night are likely so to blind one that it might not be possible to judge with the necessary precision one's distance from the barge and the bank, and a few feet in error either way could have very serious results. So we never travelled at night.

On the Waterway all opening bridges are manned day and night, and at all but a few near the Cape Kennedy rocket complex, and near Fort Lauderdale and Miami, water traffic, no matter how small and unimportant, has the right of way. Often the bridge tender sees one approaching and opens up without being asked, but if he does not, one has only to give three long blasts on the foghorn to cause bells to ring, red lights to flash, and barriers to drop, stacking up cars and trucks on either hand; then the span swings slowly open, or the bascules lift to let one pass with a glow of self-importance. We remained for a day at Fairfield, as we wished to make a movie sequence of the swing bridge in operation. There were five tenders taking single-handed watches in turn, and I fear that they did not approve of our filming, for movie-making involves much watching, waiting, and rehearsal, and I believe they thought we were up to no good, for when I called on the tender after dark to have a yarn in his warm cabin on the span, he said he was too busy, though with what I did not know, as he sat in semi-darkness and there was no canal traffic that night.

Bridges and waterborne traffic had been causing us some anxiety ever since we entered the Waterway, because our motor had taken to stopping without warning due to lack of fuel. As this could, and sometimes did, happen at awkward moments, such as when a fair current was hurrying us towards a bridge which had not yet started to open, or while we were being

◀

34. *Top:* The commercial traffic on the Waterway, barges pushed by blunt-bowed tugs, is so skilfully handled that it presents no real hazard to small craft in daylight. *Bottom:* Nevertheless it was pleasant to watch the traffic go by from the security of our berth in the cross-canal at Fairfield Bridge.

overtaken, we were on tenterhooks. The stoppages were due not to dirty fuel but to air-locks, which I could neither account for or prevent until we met along the way a friendly boatbuilder from the Chesapeake, a Mr. Dickerson. He suggested that the fuel pipes might have become bent or kinked over the years, and advised me to fit new and larger ones. After I had done so we never again suffered from air-locks; the beautifully made little Stuart Turner ran faultlessly and almost as quietly as a sewing machine and we had a wonderfully relaxed feeling—indeed, until that point we had not realized quite how delightful much of the trip could be.

The Waterway, having started in Virginia, runs through four states: North Carolina, South Carolina, Georgia, and Florida, and I think ours must have been the slowest vessel on it, for we took 46 days (we were under way on 41 of them) over a trip which is often done in 10 or less, and not only pusher tugs with their barges, but mobile houseboats and amphibious cars easily overtook us. However, we had been told that the Waterway leads through some of the wildest and least-known parts of the country, and we were determined to see as much as possible of it; also we wanted to experience life in marinas and meet our fellow travellers.

While we were in North Carolina the weather was often bad; small-craft warnings (these are issued when winds of 33 knots are forecast) were common; but except in the more open stretches this did not bother us. However, it was cold, and often there was ice on deck when we turned out to make an early start in the morning. So we moved on as fast as we could then to keep ahead of winter, which was hard on our heels chasing us south. But usually the wind was fair, as is to be expected at that time of year. Most of our stops in that state were at 'tie-ups' of one sort or another, but in South Carolina and Georgia we did not feel so pressed, and were able to explore some of the rivers and creeks which lead off the Waterway or bypass sections of it. The charts give soundings in many of these, but we found that at the mouth of every one we entered or tried to enter there was less water than charted, due to silting since the original survey

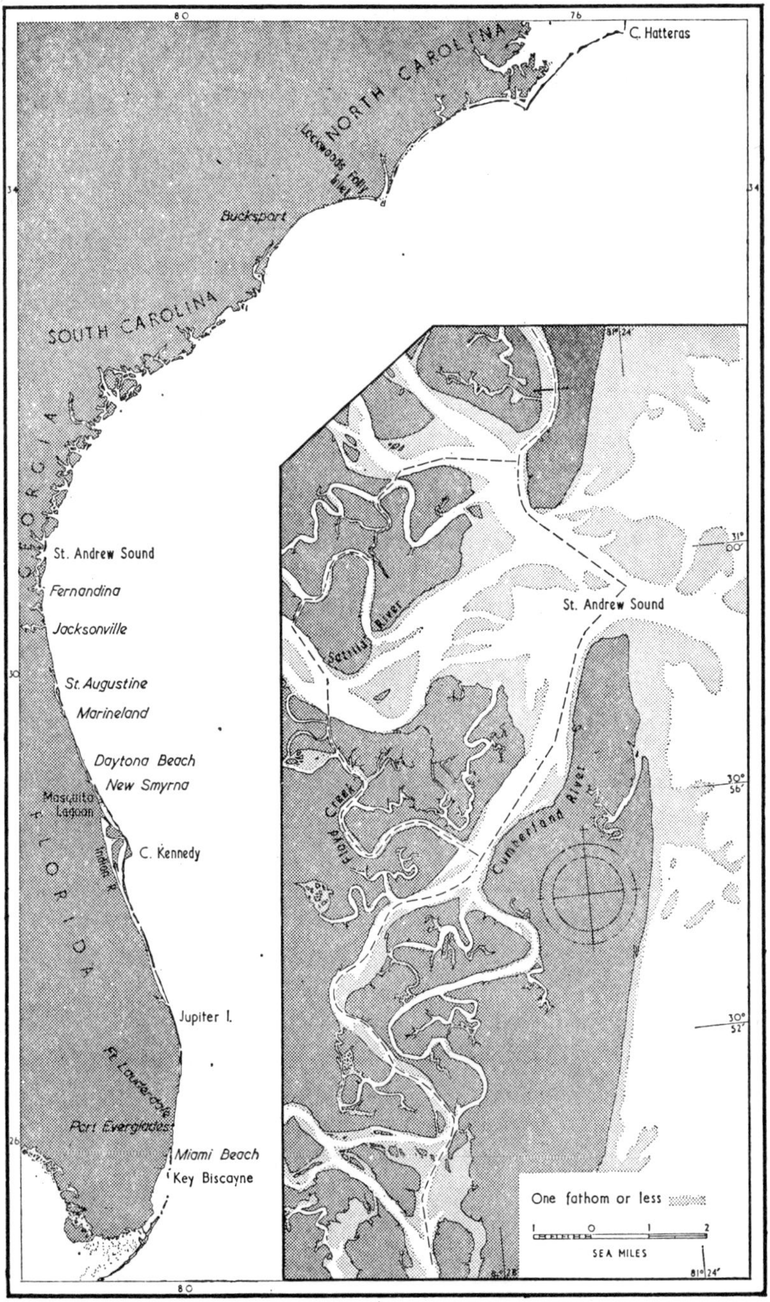

EAST COAST OF UNITED STATES

from Cape Hatteras to Key Biscayne with larger-scale inset of part of the Intra-coastal Waterway in the neighbourhood of St. Andrew Sound was made; however, we touched such bars only on a few occasions, and always got off without difficulty. Out of our total of 46 nights we spent 20 at anchor, some of them in the most perfectly protected and peaceful berths imaginable. Often these were in offshoots of the Waterway or behind small islands in it, sheltered by trees, which in the northern part of South Carolina were hung with Spanish moss, a parasite plant which because of its grey colour gives the impression that the trees are dead or blighted. It was remarkable how suddenly we came into that area; north of a bridge near Bucksport the trees looked normal, but south of it the Spanish moss hung everywhere. Also in that area we saw on the trunks of fallen trees at the water's edge what at first we took to be toadstools, but which proved to be turtles, sometimes as many as a dozen on one tree. Other anchorages were among the marsh islands, and unless one climbed aloft to look for distant land, there was nothing to be seen except winding creeks and marsh grass, golden in the sunshine, whispering in the breeze; alligators there may have been, though we did not see any until we were in Florida; the only creatures we did see there were birds, among them gulls, oyster-catchers, herons, duck, and pelicans. Sometimes from such anchorages we could hear the rumble of surf, for much of the Waterway is separated from the ocean only by a narrow strip of land or white dunes. There are many inlets from the ocean, though only a few are navigable, and where the Waterway crosses one of these breakers can often be seen on the shoals, and the swift tidal streams need watching or they may carry one out of the channel and put one ashore.

It was in such a place, Lockwood's Folly Inlet, that we had our only real stranding. The Waterway is well marked by beacons, distinctive in colour and shape, many are lighted, while there are often sets of range markers in awkward places. But these alone are not sufficient to keep one in deep water everywhere, for not always is it safe to steer direct from one ▶

35. *Top:* At Norfolk, Virginia, the busy naval and commercial port, two bridges, road and rail, lift their bascules to let us through. *Bottom:* A swing bridge on the Waterway closes astern of us.

beacon to the next without consulting the chart, as the channel may take a curved course there. We knew that was how most yachts get into trouble, so we made frequent reference to the chart, which was either on the bridge deck or in the helmsman's hand, and on this occasion we noticed a pencilled remark made by one of the friends who had 'briefed' us for the trip:

'Build-out,' it said. 'Favor the western side.' So we did that, and immediately ran hard aground on sand. This was in one of the rare places where there is much range of tide, and had the water-level been falling this could have been awkward in that somewhat exposed position; but fortunately the tide was rising, and after launching the dinghy and laying out the kedge, we did not have to wait long until we could pull ourselves off.

In a few places there are alternative routes to the main Waterway, and we were glad to make use of one of these when we were approaching St. Andrew Sound. The section copied from a typical Waterway chart, and inset on page 119, shows that to avoid some shoals in the sound the dashed line of the Waterway channel goes almost out to sea, and the day we were in the area there was a strong east wind and tides were at the top of springs. Therefore, seeing no reason for making ourselves wet and uncomfortable (you see how soft we were becoming) we turned inland before reaching the sound, and took the delightfully narrow, twisting creeks (stopping in one of them for lunch) which lead to the Satilla river; this we crossed, and then plunged into another network of creeks, and as night was falling anchored in Floyd Creek. We were glad to be in such a snug berth when after dark the wind freshened into a gale, and we remained there all the next day, but had to keep the cooker going to hold the temperature up to 50°F., even though we were in latitude 31 degrees north, for winter had already laid his icy hands on the country, and inland and to the north of us there had been great storms with many inches of snow, and even north

◀

36. *Top:* A lift bridge raises its span at our signal, and, *bottom,* we hope the bridge tender has judged the height of our mast correctly and lifted his span enough to clear it.

Florida had frost forecast for that night. When the wind veered and moderated we continued on our way and rejoined the main Waterway channel in the Cumberland river.

Perhaps because of the novelty, we enjoyed stopping at marinas almost as much as we enjoyed the lonely anchorages among the marsh islands, and in Florida we had to use them nearly every night because of the lack of good anchorages. Usually we made an early start either before or immediately after breakfast, and tried to select in advance a marina which we could be sure of reaching by mid-afternoon; if we arrived late there was a risk of finding it full, for we were going down the Waterway at a busy time of year when thousands of power yachts from the north were heading south for winter sunshine. But unless a marina had been specially recommended to us by a recent user, our selection was something of a gamble, for although the chart folder lists all marinas on that chart, gives the depth in the approach and alongside, and states what fuels and facilities are available, it can, of course, give no hint as to the atmosphere and quality of the place, neither does it say anything about cost. We found that the charge varied from 10*s.* to 35*s.* a night, and tended to increase the farther south we went, though the services and facilities did not necessarily bear any relation to the charge. For this one is given a berth alongside, and if there is more than a foot or so of tidal range, the berth will probably be at a pontoon, known as a 'float', so that one can step ashore with ease at any time and never have to make any adjustment to the dock lines. At some marinas the entire establishment, berths, fuel pumps, office, showers, and even the roof protecting motor cruisers from the sun, rises and falls with the tide.

The berth is almost invariably provided with fresh water and usually with an electric power point. This last is essential for the majority of power yachts which use the Waterway, for what with refrigeration, deep-freeze, cooking, lighting, air-conditioning, and television, many are so dependent on electricity that either they must run a generator all the time or else plug in, and a few we met apparently needed to do both. Marinas also provide all or some of the following: hot showers and compartments marked 'buoys' and 'gulls', or sometimes carrying a picture of a light-vessel with the word 'relief' on her side; a rest and television lounge (we found it difficult to reconcile these two requirements); a coin-operated laundromat, a marine store, and often either a provision shop or a free car to take one to town. This sort of thing makes life afloat so effortless that Susan and I have sometimes wondered how the American yachtsman manages when cruising in European waters, where there are so few tie-ups offering the facilities to which he is accustomed, and where he must often have to ferry water out from the shore, something we never had to do all the time we were in America. There was a time when Waterway marinas made no charge for one night's dockage provided the yacht bought fuel, but not now, though presumably much of a marina's income does come from the sale of fuel. Sometimes we have stood by a pump in the evening when one of the power yachts was 'gassing up' for the next day's run, and have watched with amazement the figures rise to several hundred gallons. Our own request for four gallons, enough to keep our tiny engine running for eight hours, was sometimes treated with hilarity, but never with contempt.

We did not often see another sailing yacht, but usually shared the marinas with smart, well-handled power yachts which, immediately on arrival, and having plugged in and turned off their motors, were hosed down all over with fresh water. For the most part they lacked nothing, and the expensive business of keeping up with the Joneses was much in evidence, but to our way of thinking it was odd that the owners of such costly, handsome, and efficient vessels should display so strange a sense of humour when naming them. Some of the names, taken from Susan's diary, are: *Miss Print*, *Miss Deed*, *Miss Take*, *Foo-Ling-U*, *Rocky Dame*, *Blood Vessel*, *I. M. Foresail*, *Mr. Ree*, *Don't Barge*, *Glug Glug* (I believe this one did eventually sink in the Bahamas), *Rusty Boy*. Perhaps we should name our new vessel *Seacock*! We found their people friendly and interested, some expressed amazement that we had crossed the Atlantic in 'that little bitty boat', and often they invited us aboard for a drink and a yarn; when after dark we made our way back along the dock where all that wealth of boats lay, we could see through deckhouse windows figures gathered round the cold blue flicker of the television screens, the tall lampshades, the cocktail cabinets, like a scene from a silent movie, for no sound penetrated the air-conditioning seals.

Soon after dawn there was a roar of warming up motors, and quickly our friends of the evening vanished out of sight ahead, leaving us to be overtaken presently by what we referred to as the 'pack of hounds', the bunch of power yachts which had spent the night at some marina we had passed the previous day, all hell-bent for Daytona Beach, Fort Lauderdale, or Miami; but no matter how urgent was their business always they slowed so as not to inconvenience us with their wash, and to give a wave and a shouted greeting. And so day followed day as we progressed to the south, the helmsman with peaked cap pulled well down to shade his eyes from the now powerful sun, which always seemed to be ahead. In the stretches of narrow canal there was nothing much to do except keep clear of the banks and other craft, but in the wider stretches, such as the Indian river and Mosquito Lagoon, each beacon and buoy had to be identified well in advance, and Susan, because she sees so well, bore the brunt of that. It was fun, it was rewarding, but it was tiring, and we were never sorry to pull into a marina in the afternoon with sunburnt faces, have a shower, and relax for a little before doing our homework for the next day's run.

Although Florida is the least attractive of the Waterway states, it provides plenty of contrasts to entertain strangers like us. Immediately within its border stands the town of Fernandina, its paper mills belching smoke, and their stench is mixed with that from the fish fertilizer establishments. The only bright thing seen there was the 'welcome station', where the visitor is invited to tie up in the tideway on a lee shore and accept a glass of cold orange juice 'on the State'. We gave it a careful look and then went on to a first-class marina near Jacksonville, and took a taxi into the city to get our cruising permit renewed. Our driver said he was saving up to buy a 40-foot power yacht to take his wife down to the West Indies. From the marina we walked a mile or so along the road to Jacksonville Beach to see what a Florida seaside resort looked like, but we were too late in the year. At its end the road widened and was fringed with many gas stations and second-hand car lots, each complete with strings of tattered bunting and festoons of coloured lights, and between them were squeezed in several eating places, but there were no dwellings. Beyond, an incline ran down into the ocean where among the breakers stood a notice which read: 'Speed limit 10 m.p.h.' On a little wooden stand under an umbrella sat a beach guard, sound asleep. There was nobody else around.

On the straight bit of Waterway south of Jacksonville the chart indicates a marina, but we found its notices flaking and unreadable, and its dock, staggering out from the shore, looked ready to fall at a touch. At its root an old man with clothes as grey and worn as his shack was hammering at something, and as we passed he turned his back, and without the wave which most Waterway people give, limped to his doorway. Perhaps many years ago he had the idea of serving the stream of transient yachts with fuel and other things, and had built the place with his small savings and his own labour, only to watch the yachts pass by bound for glossier marinas.

St. Augustine, the nation's oldest city, stands within one of the navigable ocean inlets. On approaching it we had to pass a lift bridge, and on leaving it a bascule bridge, and the mile and a half of water which lay between was full of life and colour. The red and black buoys leant steeply to the inrushing tide, which did its utmost to set us off our course; seaward breakers curled white and angry on the shoals; landward lay a white sandbank almost awash, and over this a great gathering of birds wheeled and cried; ahead of us a school of porpoises leapt and plunged, and beyond towered the great 19-mile lighthouse, clad surprisingly in sweeping black and white spirals. The city with its flat red roofs, its spires, its fort, clearly showed its Spanish origin.

Marineland, the big aquarium on the seaward side of the Waterway south of St. Augustine, is famous for its performing porpoises, the bottlenose kind with the built-in grin, which leap through hoops, play water polo, and tow little boats with dogs on board, apparently doing these things with great good humour. We stopped at Marineland's convenient tie-up to have a look, and were, of course, delighted with the performance of the jolly, warm-blooded porpoises, but were more interested in watching the other deep-sea creatures through the windows low down in the huge, well-lit tanks. There were sharks, sting rays, saw-fish, turtles, and all manner of other creatures living in harmony together (perhaps because they were kept well fed), and an excellent commentary came over the undistorted public address system. The Americans do know how to provide the little touches to make life comfortable and convenient; here, for example, just in case the visitor wants to go out and buy more film, or return to his yacht for a meal or a rest, when he first pays for admission the back of his hand is marked with an indelible date stamp, so that for the rest of that day he can come or go as he pleases without having to make further payment.

At the Daytona Beach Municipal Marina we found few transients, but many inhabited yachts already settled in for the winter, that being a favourite end to the autumn trek south for some who go there year after year, and it was full. But among them we found friends who managed to obtain a berth for us, as one of the permanent residents was on the slip for painting. However, we much preferred the simple little marina 30 miles on at New Smyrna, close beside the fish dock used by a fleet of cocky shrimp boats which work the sounds and the shoals off the coast. The compact and friendly town was conveniently close, and we were so impressed with the vast, spotless supermarket, and the luxurious bank, which had fitted, deep-pile carpets, a lounge provided with the latest magazines, and soft music, that we spent a day making a movie sequence, ably assisted by the bank staff. Also the press got hold of us there, and some time later we received a folder on which was printed:

'You're news . . . and we were delighted to read about you. All of us at the Bank of New Smyrna extend our sincerest good wishes.' Within it was a cutting from the paper. Nicholson, even though he did get bedaylighted and had to be rescued once, thought New Smyrna was a good place; he spent his nights aboard the shrimp boats, from which he returned smelling strongly of fish and Cuprinol.

Although in America we got used to many things that were at first strange to us, there were two which continued to the end to astonish us: the Sunday papers, and packaging. One typical paper, which cost 25 cents, contained 258 full-size pages in fifteen sections with such headings as Fashion, Home, Local News, Sport, Viewpoint, Arts, Travel, and two sections of Comic Strips; there were also eighty-eight pages in tabloid form in six sections. Just to handle this without reading any of it is quite a formidable Sunday task. In the supermarkets, such as the one we had just visited at New Smyrna, every soft, sliced loaf (they don't seem to understand about baking crusty bread, and all of it is purified or fortified or made tasteless in one way or another) is in its own transparent bag, as, indeed, are most things which are not in cartons with glowing pictures on them; sliced bacon (smoky and thin, and the best we have had in any country) is sold in a box with a plastic window, and even tomatoes, four at a time, come in a plastic tray wrapped in cellophane; a pound of butter when unwrapped is found to be in four separately packaged fingers, and chocolate, wafer thin, is double wrapped in ounces; at the cashier's booth one stout brown paper bag is thrust within another before one's purchases are stowed inside. We found the disposal of so many wrappings (and the Sunday paper) quite a problem in a country where nothing is ever thrown overboard, and wondered what the housewife, whose collection must be so much greater than ours, does with hers.

During our final three days of the run down to Fort Lauderdale the scene steadily became more southern, with many palms, and brilliant, almost Bahamian, colouring; it also became more sophisticated. On Jupiter Island stood many fine homes, beautifully landscaped, each with its dock at which a smart yacht lay; and as we passed the golf course we could watch the players driving in small cars with high white canopies from one lie to the next. In and around Fort Lauderdale land values are high, and even land which is under water comes on the market, is bought and reclaimed. We passed through areas which were being developed, where from among a herd of loud-voiced earth-moving machines, multi-storied apartment blocks thrust their blunt heads into the clear blue sky. We wondered who would want to go and live in them, and why. On we went past thousands of white and colour-washed holiday homes, many looking like meat-safes because of their insect screens, each, of course, with its motor cruiser, sport fisherman, or speed-boat lying at the bottom of the garden near the sunken, floodlit swimming pool. Waterway traffic grew heavier as we neared the centre of the city, and we began to think that some form of traffic control was necessary at the narrower places and blind corners, and were not sorry to tie up at the Bahia Mar, which is said to be the largest marina in the country.

This, of course, has every facility, including its own shopping area complete with post office and beauty salon, and on the land mass at its centre a new motel was to be opened that very evening. We were invited to the inaugural cocktail party, so we got out our slightly musty finery and went along to sample the scotch and bourbon, and to watch the women making their rounds with intense concentration as they piled their plates with layer upon layer of the excellent 'eats'. Afterwards we took a walk across the wide A1A, where the traffic snarled, to the beach beyond. Behind us lay civilization with its petrol fumes and smell of French fry, the sunblinds at the floodlit shop windows beating and snatching at their supports in the fresh north-east wind, the garish, green strip-lights of the motel. The beach was empty of all but the day's million footprints in the sand, and above it the palm fronds leaned and rustled in the breeze. We walked down to the dim, grey line of the surf, and

▶

37. Most of the marinas at which we stopped were packed with well-kept power yachts and sport fishermen, and if the range of tide was more than a foot or two, the entire establishment was floating and free to rise and fall with it. *Bottom:* Sometimes we shared a berth with the prawners which work the sounds and off-shore shoals of Georgia and Florida.

looking out beyond it saw the old, wild Atlantic, black and empty under a pall of cloud. Shivering a little, though the night was not cold, we retraced our steps and went out along Pier B, past the Christmas trees and coloured lights with which some of the yachts and their docks had been decorated, and back to *Wanderer*'s homely cabin, thankful that not this night, nor for many nights, need we think of heading out to sea.

For a stranger unwilling to face the expense and the crowded conditions of a marina, this area presents something of a problem if he wishes to stay, as we did, for more than a few days, because there are no anchorages. However, with typical American understanding and hospitality a voyaging couple, Bob and Mary Kittredge, owners of the yacht *Svea*, had invited us through our mutual friends Van and Jo Vancil of *Rena* (you may remember that we met them at Madeira) to go to their private lagoon at Fort Lauderdale and stay there as long as we wished. So the next morning with chart in hand we cautiously made our way up the New River to look for it. We understood then why Fort Lauderdale is often called the Venice of America; lagoons, canals, and creeks branched off in all directions so that a moment's inattention could get one lost, and there were hair-pin bends with closed bridges lurking round them, and a constant stream of traffic. But all went well, and 4 miles up the river we recognized *Rena*'s graceful clipper bow among the trees; close to her lay a double-ended ketch with the name *Svea* on her stern, and just beyond was David Robertson's little *Vagabond*. At our hail their people all came running to take our lines and warp us gently in to the most perfect little lagoon we had ever seen, lying crooked in repose as a reminder of South Florida's pioneer days, when land was developed for pure beauty instead of developer footage; it was about 100 yards long and only 40 to 70 feet wide. They made fast our lines to four royal palms so that our bow and stern were only a few feet from the grass which surrounded us, and we stepped ashore to meet our hosts.

◀
38. *Top:* A lonely anchorage among the marsh islands of South Carolina, with little to be seen but winding creeks and marsh grass, golden in the sunshine. *Bottom:* Egrets line a marsh island in the early-morning sunshine.

Dark-bearded Bob, and his tall and charming Mary with her lovely southern drawl, were both professional sculptors, and two of Bob's architectural granite reliefs measuring 11 ft by 8 ft are above the doors of the Railroad Retirement Board's building facing the Capitol in Washington, D.C. After they got married they built, largely with their own hands and to their own designs, a colony of artistic homes in a remarkable hillside position at Flagstaff in Arizona, and leased them to discerning people. In 1961, although I believe they had never before been out of sight of land, they decided to make a long voyage; they bought the Danish-built ketch *Svea*, and setting out from California, sailed west-about to reach Fort Lauderdale four years later. It was then the beginning of the hurricane season, and seeking a safe berth for *Svea* while they visited their property in Arizona, they went one day by outboard dinghy up the New River and found this lagoon. Seeing a man sitting in front of the house, Bob asked him if he knew who the owner was.

'I am the owner,' was the reply.

'Suppose you wouldn't think of selling the place?'

'Sure would.' And Bob bought it, not just for his own use, but so that he and Mary could invite their voyaging friends along to enjoy it, too.

The Vancils had been there about a year when we arrived, indeed, ever since they returned from their European voyage, and David Robertson in *Vagabond* had been there about six months. He had experienced some bad luck. During his single-handed crossing from Madeira to Grenada a masthead fitting had carried away, and as a result the passage took over 40 days. More recently, while lying in this sheltered lagoon, which is the last place one might have expected such a thing to happen, a tree blew down in a gale and fell on top of his little vessel, smashing her mast and bowsprit, among other things. He was now busy, under Van's supervision, making good the damage, for he wanted to get to the Bahamas to meet his son and daughter-in-law in the spring.

Van, who had been a flying man and an engineer in the Navy, and had, as I have mentioned earlier, with Jo's assistance built their lovely *Rena* without any outside help and even made the metal fittings for her, was now giving Bob a hand to build an hydraulic-electric steering gear which he had invented, for Bob and Mary were planning more voyages, and like us after our second long trip had grown tired of having to steer by hand.

I found it hard to believe that both Mary and Jo were grandmothers, for, as I recall, grannies in my day were always very old and lined, and usually wore long, black skirts and velvet ribbons round their emaciated necks. Today's grannies, or at least the voyaging kind that we have met, possess long, slender, sun-tanned legs, and run about in brief shorts or even in bikinis, and look enchanting. Could this be because today women become grannies earlier, or is it simply that they refuse to grow old?

Like our friends, we had work to do aboard the ship, but Susan attended to most of that while I settled down with my typewriter to revise one of my textbooks and make a start on this one. We could not have found a better place for these jobs, for all day our companions were busy about their own business, and unless we asked for help or advice they never disturbed us. But Van, who is a perfectionist and a glutton for work, did keep Bob and David hard at it, overseeing efficiently the work they did, discarding it, and sometimes even tossing it contemptuously into the lagoon if it failed to reach a sufficiently high standard.

'You have got to live with it,' I heard him say one day to David, who was fitting his new bowsprit and had not got it steeved up enough. 'Come and view it from over here and judge for yourself if you can bear to look at the damn thing year after year.'

But every evening we all gathered in the Kittredge home for a drink and to discuss the day's doings and our plans for the future. The little brown house (the front veranda had been turned for the time being into a workshop) was cosy and intimate, and on evenings when a sudden strong norther bent the heads of the palms and the casuarinas, we did not have the usual pang of anxiety lest our floating home might drag her anchor, or that some other vessel might collide with her, for within a few yards of us the four yachts lay securely moored in water with scarcely a ripple on it; nor was there now any risk from falling trees, for after the accident to *Vagabond* any trees likely to be dangerous had been severely lopped.

Bob, a skilful raconteur, spun one of his hilarious yarns if ever the conversation flagged, Van slowly slapping his thigh in approval like a Fijian at a kava-drinking, but on the stroke of seven o'clock marched with his glass to the sink while Jo packed up her knitting, and the party was over.

'You mustn't go yet,' cried Mary, 'or my face will be loong like that of a doorg.' But we did go, for we all rose early in the morning, and there would be many more evening gatherings to enjoy.

We were looked after extremely well. Bob and Van rigged us up with mains electric light and a fan, and there was a fresh-water tap within reach of our hose, while ashore there were showers and refrigerators for our use, and a lift to the shopping centre and laundromat any time we wanted one. There were squirrels in the trees, rabbits on the lawns, and in the lagoon fish which sometimes a heron caught and left on the bank all handy for Nicholson's breakfast. The only unwelcome creatures were ants, which unnoticed by us must have made their industrious but hazardous way aboard along one of our mooring lines, for we found large numbers of them in dark places, in the ventilator traps and cockpit locker drains, and even in bags of sails. Spraying with insecticide killed some, but they were a hardy breed and must have brought supplies of food along with them, for we continued to find live ants aboard from that time on, and a few even got into our house six months later when we took our gear ashore at the end of the voyage.

At least once a week all of us dined in the house on a meal provided by one or other of the yachts, and just occasionally we ate in some restaurant in town, for Bob loved dining out. One evening after drinks in the slowly revolving tower of the Pier 66

▶

39. *Top:* Four miles up the New River we found the Kittredge lagoon with the ketch *Svea* lying in front of the little house, and, *bottom*, met our hosts, Bob and Mary, who had bought the place at the end of their circumnavigation, and . . .

Marina and a meal ashore with Bob and Mary only, for David was unwell and the Vancils were away, we went on to the Bahia Mar to have a look at the yachts and see if any newcomers had arrived. We were making our way out along Pier B, where only a short time before *Wanderer* had lain, when we came to a piece of rope with a red flag on it strung across a foot or so above the planking. Susan and Mary, who were a little ahead of Bob and me, were just stepping over this obstruction so as to look at the dozen or so yachts beyond, when a woman screamed at them from the deck of a motor cruiser:

'Out. Out. Out. Get out. I won't have you spying on me.'

Susan and Mary stopped in astonishment, and Bob and I caught up with them.

'But, madam,' said Bob in his courteous manner, 'surely this dock belongs not to you but Bahia Mar.'

'Don't you speak to me like that, you bastard. Get out, the lot of you.' And as she rushed at him Bob took off his glasses and carefully put them in his shirt pocket. Mary seized the woman by the hair.

The next person to arrive on the scene was what we took to be the husband, threatening to use his gun on us. I, hating a drunken scene more than most, took Mary by the arm and tried to lead her away; but she shook me off, for she had no intention of abandoning her Bob. Susan meanwhile quietly removed the rope with its flag and bronze cliphooks, and dropped it in the water, where it sank immediately.

Eventually we got away, fortunately without a shot being fired or any harm being done, and the last words we heard were:

'I'll have the police on you.'

She did, too, and we were still on Pier B having a talk with a man who had just brought his sailing yacht down the Waterway, when there was a whine of sirens, and we found ourselves suddenly surrounded by smart, revolver-carrying cops, just like on the movies, and within a few minutes were at the police

◀

40. . . . there among the trees *Wanderer* lay in the most perfect little nook she had ever seen, while Susan attended to her needs and I did my writing.

station, where I derived wicked pleasure from holding open the swing door to let the plaintiffs in.

The police, I thought, were not taking this little matter too seriously, but they did want to know just who we were.

To Bob: 'You say you are Robert Kittredge and live with your wife up the New River. Can you prove it?' Then, turning to me: 'You, sir, claim to be British, and you sure talk that way. Can you show me your immigration card?' But, of course, I had not got it with me.

Then Bob had an idea. 'Do you have a copy of today's *Miami Herald* here?'

They said they thought so, and sent to fetch it.

Bob opened it at the peach-coloured magazine section and showed them the two-page spread which by chance had appeared that day. There were large pictures of the yachts in the Kittredge lagoon and portraits of their people, together with a long article about us all.

That appeared to satisfy the police, and as we shook hands with them the senior one drew me aside, and with a touch of the Irish in his voice whispered:

'I reckon this is all your fault, dad. It's time you learnt not to accost strange women, specially when they're high.'

We drove home then, and it was good after the close, disinfected atmosphere of the police station to feel the clean night air on our faces, and to see as we came to the end of the winding drive the yachts lying peacefully in the moonlit lagoon. We whispered our 'good nights' so as not to disturb David, whose light was out, and quietly went on board.

Our time at the lagoon passed all too quickly, and the weeks had lengthened into nearly three months before we had completed our work. The day we left Susan and I could hardly control our voices sufficiently to say good-bye, Bob was gruff, and Mary was in tears.

9

NORTH ATLANTIC

We had planned our homeward voyage by way of the Bahamas (again), Bermuda, Azores, and south-west Ireland, a total distance of some 4,500 miles, and hoped to reach England in July to attend to the designing and building of *Wanderer IV*, a larger vessel to be our permanent cruising home.

Through the 50-mile-wide gap between Florida and the Bahamas runs the Gulf Stream, which along its axis attains a speed of 4 knots; but taking into consideration the lesser speed each side of the axis, it is customary to allow for an average north-setting stream of 2½ knots when crossing it in that area. The shortest crossing to Great Isaac light (see chart on page 70), which we intended to leave to starboard on our way to Nassau, and so keep in deep water instead of crossing the northern end of the Great Bahama Bank, as yachts with shallow draught often do, is from Fort Lauderdale's harbour, Port Everglades. But having made our way down the winding New River into more open country, we found unsuitable conditions for attempting the crossing, as the wind was light and dead ahead. Therefore, instead of putting to sea we turned south and made our way down the remaining 25-mile stretch of Inland Waterway towards Miami, the 'magic city' of the radio announcers. The power yachts and sport fishermen hurried by, their mingling wakes splashing and sucking at the banks; the bridges stopped their streams of traffic and lifted their bascules at our signal to let our tall mast through; the man-made lagoons opened up long and straight each side to reveal for a moment their neat rows of docks and houses as we slipped by. In the afternoon we passed the tight-packed skyscraper hotels fighting for footroom on the narrow strip of Miami Beach, and came to a landlocked anchorage in an empty harbour near the southern tip of Key Biscayne. The large-scale up-to-date U.S. chart gave no name to this place and showed no water in it, but as we found not less than 2 fathoms there, we presumed it had recently been dredged. That day we had passed nineteen bridges (our biggest score ever), making a total of 124 since entering the Waterway at Norfolk, and 151 since we arrived in the U.S.A. We thought our harbour a useful place for the Bahamas-bound yacht, as it is more comfortable than some of Miami's expensive marinas, and is away from the roar of traffic; also it is well placed for the crossing, being 25 miles upstream of Great Isaac, and close to a way out to the ocean; but that is a channel we would not wish to attempt again, for we found it very shallow and exposed.

In the evening the sloop *Interlude* came in and anchored, and her owners, two women doctors who had brought her down from Philadelphia, called on us. They said they had sold everything to buy *Interlude* to be their permanent home, and were now bound for St. Croix, one of the American Virgins, where posts at the hospital awaited them. Apart from the journey down the Waterway they had little boating experience, and no practical knowledge of navigation.

'Isn't that rather a difficult trip,' asked Susan as she stirred the sugar into the rum punch. 'All of it to windward unless you get a norther?'

'Oh! we'll stop by on the way at lots of the Bahamas and in Puerto Rico,' one of the doctors replied.

I do not like discouraging people or telling them what I consider they should do, but as they had brought one of my textbooks to be autographed, I chanced it.

'If I were making that trip,' I said, 'I wouldn't beat down through the islands, which are poorly lit and have unpredictable currents; I would stand out to sea from Nassau on the

▶

41. *A:* Nicholson charging batteries in his basket at the foot of the mast. *B:* Shore leave. *C:* Seeing 'em off. *D:* China cat.

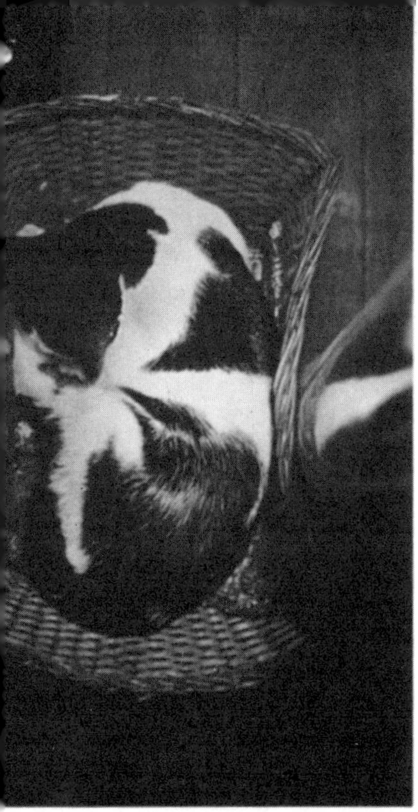

starboard tack until I thought I could fetch the Virgins on the other tack, and then go about. Bermuda might even be a convenient stop.'

We did not see the doctors again, but we often thought of them when the east wind blew hard, and we were sad to learn later that they ran ashore on one of the southern Bahamas, where their compact little floating home became a total loss.

Our crossing of the Gulf Stream was uneventful. There was not a breath of wind as we headed east under power across its oily-smooth water, and the calm continued all day. If there were no current, that easterly course would have taken us to Gun Cay on the western edge of Great Bahama Bank, but, as expected, the northerly set averaged 2½ knots, so that at dusk we made our desired landfall on Great Isaac. We gave the light a respectable berth, and then, picking up a light fair wind, stopped the motor and during the night sailed slowly through the North-West Providence Channel towards the next turning-point, Great Stirrup light, 65 miles farther on. But three passenger ships passing well to the south of us showed that we were farther north than I thought, and we altered course more to the south to allow for the current, which obviously was still strong although we were in the lee of the bank. But even so we had to fix our position next day by observations of the sun before we could find Great Stirrup, and in the afternoon we entered Great Harbour, of which that island forms one side, and which is the northernmost anchorage in the chain of Berry Islands. The place is shallow, and twice we ran aground before reaching our chosen anchorage near the lighthouse, for we were unable to judge the depth of water within an inch or two by the colour, and weed on the bottom made this even more difficult than usual. That night we were set upon by no-see-ems, tiny

◀

42. *Top:* Unable to find at Man of War a jetty strong enough to lean against, we put the ship ashore on a sandy beach, and although the range of tide was only about 3 feet, were able to paint a surprisingly large area of the copper sheathing. *Bottom:* Hopetown Harbour on Elbow Cay is dominated by the red and white striped lighthouse, which is the landfall for many vessels bound from Europe to the Gulf and Panama.

insects which can penetrate mosquito screens unless these are swabbed with paraffin (a dodge we did not know about then) and they appeared to be armed with red-hot needles. So we left in the morning, although there was no wind, and motored down the chain of Berry Islands to Little Harbour, as it was clear we could not reach Nassau that day. In the entrance lies a rock which is awash at high tide, but as the tide was low when we approached it was standing well above water with the swell breaking round it. Ahead of us an American ocean racer was also making the entrance, and to our consternation she ran right on to the rock at speed, her bow rising noticeably. I feared we might have to do something for her, though with our low power I did wonder what assistance we could possibly offer; but with the help of the swell and her own powerful motor she got off before we arrived, and apparently was undamaged.

The anchorage was so open to most points of the compass that we did not care to remain the night there, and the entrance to the nice little landlocked harbour near by was too shallow for us, as was confirmed by the ocean racing yacht which repeatedly grounded as she tried to pass through it. So after supper we cleared out (the 10-mile flashing light at the entrance was not working, and had, we learnt later when reporting it, been extinguished for some weeks) and in wonderfully smooth, phosphorescent water, with a faint air on the beam to give us steerage way, ghosted silently towards Nassau, now only 30 miles away. The sky was ablaze with stars, and we noticed that the planet Venus had won the neck-and-neck race she had been running the previous night with the sickle of the new moon.

The approach to Nassau was bewildering because of a glow of illumination which made it impossible to identify the flashing light marking the entrance; but as we drew closer we realized that two passenger ships, their decks ablaze with light, and with festoons of lights rigged from stem to stern over their mastheads, were lying at anchor outside the port. We knew they must be tourist ships, and wondered then, as we have so often wondered before, why the lovely vessels which are engaged in that trade have to doll themselves up like a fun-fair with strings of flags by day and festoons of lights by night. Until recently dressing ship overall like this was reserved for very special occasions, such as the Queen's birthday or Independence Day, but now seems to have little significance except perhaps as a signal to shopkeepers to put their prices up and stand by.

At dawn we crept into the harbour and made our way to the Yacht Haven to enter, and then went over to the Hurricane Hole Marina on Hog Island, where, in the absence of the dock-master, friends of our earlier visit directed us to a vacant berth, and we tied up to a finger pier in the oval, tree-sheltered basin. The handsome, new, steeply arched bridge, which will no doubt be the ruination of Hog Island, was nearing completion; the downtown ferry ran only when it felt like it; the washing machines displayed the notice most widely used in Nassau today: THIS MACHINE IS TEMPORARILY OUT OF ORDER; and a mechanic had taken the ice-making machine to pieces. However, the sloops from the out islands still came gaily in under sail, and the inter-island motor vessels, *Air Swift*, *Plymouth Queen*, *Noel Roberts*, *Air Pheasant*, and *Stede Bonnet*, came and went about their business.

Having attended to our affairs in the town, and having waited for two northers in quick succession to sweep through—one of these caused the total loss in the harbour mouth of *Tropic Rover*, the 150-foot catamaran which was said to be the largest in the world—we left Nassau by the back door, or eastern entrance, a place which we mistrust, as the depth of water in it appears to bear little relation to the soundings given on the chart, and due to the dark colour of the bottom we found pilotage by eye impossible. We were particularly worried on this occasion because we had to attempt it just after high water if we were to reach our destination before nightfall, and soon after passing through the Narrows the echo-sounder showed less and less water, and we did not know which way to turn to improve matters. However, more by luck than good judgement we got clear, and in deep water sailed north-east to spend several windy days in Royal Island's landlocked harbour, where the Pyes' *Moonraker* was so nearly lost on the rock in the entrance. The harbour is good, but the island is privately owned and landing is not permitted. Then we sailed on across North-East Providence Channel bound for our favourite Bahama, Man of War Cay. We intended to make our landfall on the light on Elbow Cay, 60 miles away, and to allow for the possibility of an onshore current I laid a course for a point 10 miles to seaward of the lighthouse.

After we had got clear of the land by nightfall the wind freshened from forward of the beam, and now and then the moon shone smearily through thin places in the cloud cover. With a reef rolled in the mainsail we made good but uncomfortable progress, and two hours before dawn sighted the group flash of the 14-mile light on Elbow Cay. But this proved to be on a dangerous bearing, due, no doubt, to the fact that in spite of my allowance for current we had been set a long way to the west. The sea had become confused, as though it was feeling the bottom on the edge of the bank, and the wind chose that moment to fall light, leaving us with slamming sails and bare steerage way. We then, and I believe for the first time in our sailing lives, made use of the motor at sea to help extricate us from a dangerous situation, and motor-sailing close-hauled we very slowly drew out into deep water and in time brought the light on to a safe bearing. We have since met several people who have had similar experiences of onshore currents off the eastern side of Abaco.

Our second visit to Man of War was even more enjoyable than our first one had been, for this time we were there a little earlier in the year, and several of our American friends who have holiday homes on the cay were still in residence. One couple let us have the use of their rainwater supply with which to do our laundry and fill our tanks after we had pumped out the Nassau water, which, perhaps because too much is drawn from the wells, is so hard and brackish as to be unpleasant to drink and difficult to wash in. Also there was a coming and going of yachts, including our old friends *Svea* and *Rena* from Fort Lauderdale, and *Wind's Song* from Nova Scotia, and there was a meet of the Florida Station of the Cruising Club of

America to which we were invited; throughout our stay we rarely had an evening to ourselves.

We had not scrubbed or painted *Wanderer*'s copper-sheathed bottom in the past eight months, but due to the long time she had spent in the almost fresh water of the Kittredge lagoon, there was only a little slime on it, and this we were able to wipe off while bathing. But there was not much paint left along the waterline, and we wanted to renew it because it is there that the copper gets most eroded if not protected. We examined all of the many wooden piers at Man of War, but the piles of most were rotten, and we failed to find one sufficiently strong to lean against. So, soon after high water one lovely blue and sunny morning we ran the ship ashore on the hard sand just off a friend's house, and took a line to the mangroves to hold her there. The range of tide was only about 3 feet, yet with the ship listed over to 30° we were able to antifoul a surprisingly large area down from the waterline, but, of course, to do both sides took two days. Life on board at such an angle was so inconvenient that we took a picnic lunch ashore, much to the delight of Nicholson, who liked this island, but preferred it when his owners were handy, for there are some wild cats there, and on his own he did not feel equal to disputing their territory.

We paid our last visit to the little stores in the settlement, said good-bye sadly to our friends, had one last wonderful evening with the Cooks, and on 3 May slipped for the last time out through the narrow harbour entrance and off the bank into deep water, and by noon were 20 miles on our way towards Bermuda. The weather was fine, and with the wind light and a point free, we made noon-to-noon runs in the first three days of 108, 94, and 74 miles. Then the wind started to veer and freshen, and the glass, which had been high and steady for several weeks, began to fall, a bad sign, for in low latitudes a drop in pressure usually foretells a stronger wind than does an equal drop in high latitudes. As the wind freshened so we reduced sail, and by noon of our fourth day at sea were hurrying along under the close-reefed main and small staysail, with the sea building up on the quarter. Our squeamish stomachs, quite unused to this kind of thing, contented themselves with slices of the 'outward bound' cake which Sonny Cook of *Wind's Song* had made for us, a cake which, oddly enough, is known as 'poor man's' cake in both Abaco and Nova Scotia, although those places are more than 1,000 miles apart. Nicholson, however, was undisturbed, and ate enormously, repeatedly walking to his dish of food across the body of the watch-keeper, who spent most of his or her night watches dozing on the galley floor, for we kept a 10-minute night lookout in case of meeting shipping. But the steering was done entirely by Blondie. We did not stream the patent log until towards the end of the passage, because we were in the Sargasso Sea, and there was much floating weed.

On each of the last two days of the passage we ran 142 miles, the wind blowing at between 30 and 38 knots, and the sea was rough; so great was the humidity that everything below was sticky to the touch, and the bare teak cabin sole was dark with moisture.

Standing on the edge of Plantagenet Bank, and about 25 miles south-west of Bermuda, is a Texas tower, or oil rig, and we intended to make our landfall on this. Our noon position by observations of the indistinct sun on our sixth day at sea showed that the tower lay 8 miles ahead, and sure enough we sighted it soon after, a faded yellow spider in the haze; we continued on at speed towards Bermuda, which in the late afternoon appeared on the port bow, grey and faint, when we were about 4 miles from it. Bermuda, or more correctly The Bermudas, consists of a chain of islands 14 miles long from east to west, and linked one to another by bridges; there are two main harbours: Hamilton near the west end, but with no entrance from that direction, and St. George's at the east end. To reach Hamilton we would have had to pass the entrance to St. George's, and then navigate for 15 miles or so over the bank at the northern side of the islands; so naturally we chose to put in at St. George's, which on the chart looked a good place anyway. To reach it from the direction in which we were coming we had to pass out in the open from deep water (500 fathoms) into shallow water (6 fathoms) in a distance of about 3 miles, and Susan and I wondered just what effect this sudden shoaling would have on the big sea then running when it felt the steep incline, and as night would have fallen before we reached soundings we would not be able to see if breakers lay ahead. The alternative to a night approach was to heave-to, but the lee provided by the islands is not very wide when the wind is in the south-west; also the *Pilot* made no mention of the sea being dangerous to small craft. So we held on, but with some apprehension.

Presently the air beacon and St. David's light flashed through the haze as we hurried along and made our wide sweep round the reef which lies unmarked off St. David's. Then the town lights of St. George's came into view, but were not dazzling like those of so many other ports, and in front of them we were able to pick up the dim red flash of the outer buoy; meanwhile the sea, without any apparent steepening or change of rhythm, had just flattened out. Up with the buoy we came hard on the wind and were just able to lay Town Cut, the narrow entrance channel, which is marked by several lights and some unlighted buoys, but as these are conical at *both* sides of the channel they did not help much in the dark. I felt that we had best seek an anchorage under power, for even in the lee of the land the wind was fresh, and we knew that there were some unlighted mooring buoys in the harbour. But the motor was reluctant to start, and by the time I had got it going Susan had skilfully worked the ship into the harbour, and before midnight we found an anchorage close to the southern shore, having taken 6½ days for the 750-mile passage. There was one last violent squall, a heavy shower of rain, and then all was peace.

Having made a strange port by night, it is always a thrill to see the place in daylight, and on looking out next morning we found ourselves floating in pale blue water, and on the land encircling us was a scattering of colour-washed, white-roofed houses, massing on the northern shore to form the town. We motored across and berthed at the quay on the inside of Ordnance Island alongside the friendly Dinghy and Sports Club; just across the bridge lay the jolly little town square, where stocks and pillory stand near the old town hall, and up a graceful flight of steps St. Peter's, the oldest Anglican church in continuous use in the Western Hemisphere, dominates the town.

We shared our pleasant and convenient berth with several other voyaging yachts. Among them were Jock Hardwicke's sloop *Jomada*, one of the *Wanderer* class returning to England after a West Indies cruise; *Elsie*, the 30-foot cutter in which the American Frank Casper had made a single-handed circumnavigation of the world and was now bound, still alone, for the Mediterranean; and there was the Canadian trimaran *Caravel II*, sailed by Fred and Kitty Carlisle and their two small daughters. All of these, like ourselves, intended to make Horta on the Island of Fayal (one of the Azores) their next stop. Of course, we all visited each other's vessels and had many a discussion about the 1,800-mile passage that lay ahead. Also in port was the ex-Brixham trawler *Georgiana*, on her way from the West Indies towards Maine; she had left once, but returned in a leaking condition. However, she got away a few days later, but on her way back under new ownership the following autumn she sank near Bermuda; fortunately all her people were saved.

One of my seafaring uncles in the Royal Mail Line told me that his ship took the first motor vehicle, an ambulance, to Bermuda. I cannot hold him responsible for this, for if his ship had not started the rot some other would, but I think he would be shocked if he could see the place today, with its population of 10,000 cars choking the towns and driving the cyclists off the narrow roads into the hedges or, more likely, right off the islands.

We remained for two weeks and spent most of that time at St. George's, but we did make one sortie to Hamilton, the more fashionable and sophisticated area in which the Royal Bermuda Yacht Club is situated. We went and returned by way of Ferry Reach, a short cut which is spanned by two opening road

▶

43. Close-hauled in quiet weather, and heading for Bermuda beyond the sunrise.

bridges (we had thought we had finished with bridges when we left Florida) and lay at Hamilton in the lee of White Island for two nights. The harbour and the town were full of life and colour, but our visit confirmed what the chart had already told us, that much the best place for the visiting cruising yacht is at St. George's, for at Hamilton the frequent movements of ferry boats and high-speed craft make the anchorage uneasy and dinghy work unpleasant. We were, therefore, not sorry to return to our old berth, and there, at a price, got from the friendly shopkeepers all our simple requirements. On 23 May we moved across the harbour to spend a silent night in a peaceful and attractive anchorage in Smith Sound; there we rigged up the radar reflector, bent on the weathercloths, cleaned and stowed away the dock lines, and generally prepared for sea.

For several days the glass had been falling, while humidity remained high, and the sky had a threatening aspect. But throughout our stay at Bermuda the weather had been generally out of sorts, and although Bermudans insist that good weather always starts punctually on 24 May—a public holiday when bathing commences and the fitted dinghies race—we felt we might have to wait a considerable time for an improvement. As the weather must be taken as it comes on an ocean passage, Susan and I do not consider there is anything to be gained by postponing a departure provided the wind is fair, so next morning after breakfast we left with a moderate south-west wind, and under a gloomy sky ran out through Town Cut and laid a course for the island of Fayal. On that passage there is not much difference in distance between the great circle course and the rhumb line, and we decided not to bother with the former; this proved to be just as well, for later on we had some difficulty in keeping south to the rhumb line because of winds on the starboard bow, and if we had sagged away to the north on the great

◀

44. *Top:* At St. George's we berthed alongside Ordnance Island, just across the bridge from the jolly little town square and, *bottom*, shared the harbour with several other voyaging yachts, including *Jomada* and *Elsie* (ahead and astern of *Wanderer* respectively), the Canadian trimaran *Caravel II*, and the ill-fated ex-trawler *Georgiana* (both lying at the far side).

circle course we would have had to make a tack to fetch Fayal; also, as we learnt later, we would probably have encountered a calm.

As the low, green islands of Bermuda faded quickly away into the haze astern, we could not help but wonder what the ocean held in store for us, as in most accounts that we had read of Atlantic crossings in those latitudes, even when made during the months of June and July, which have the lowest gale percentages of the year, bad weather figured largely. And we did not have long to wait for our first little bit of bad weather, for during our second night out the wind freshened from the south and raised so steep a sea that we snugged down to the deeply reefed mainsail and small staysail, and soon after made a further reduction of sail and hove-to for 12 hours, after which heavy rain killed the wind.

During the third evening at sea a remarkable thing happened; we sighted away to the north Frank Casper's *Elsie*, which had left St. George's three hours before us. With night coming on we did wonder a little about the risk of collision with her, for Frank had told us that it was his habit to look out only every three hours or so, and that the white light he exhibited was not very powerful and often blew out. However, it did then seem that we were drawing ahead of *Elsie*. We did not see her again, and it was not until after our return to England that we learnt that she took the great circle course and ran into an exasperating calm which we were fortunate enough to miss; she reached Horta 5 days after us, arriving on the same day that we left that port. Next day the wind freshened again, and under the mainsail with twelve rolls in it we made a day's run of 126 miles, which was only 10 miles less than our best day's run of that passage—rough but magnificent sailing.

Navigation presented no problem, for although there was much cloud it was possible to get morning and noon observations of the sun most days, though often these were hurried snapshots when the sun shone momentarily. There is, as I am sure most ocean voyagers know, a radio station with the call sign WWV, which gives the time, accurate to one-tenth of a second, in clear language and in morse every 5 minutes throughout the 24 hours on 2·5, 5, 10, 15 and 20 megacycles per second. On earlier voyages we had made frequent use of this for the purpose of checking the chronometer; but during the previous winter the station was moved from its old position on the east coast of the U.S.A. to Fort Collins in Colorado, and since then we had found it impossible to pick up in daylight, and only occasionally and rather faintly during the hours of darkness. However, on this passage the B.B.C. World Service came in loud and clear in the morning and evening and often at other times, and we made use of the time signals given on it. We continued to listen for entertainment to the medium-wave stations at Bermuda, and so learnt of the failure of one yacht to arrive there, and of another which, after an extensive air/sea search had been organized, reported that she had a choked fuel pipe.

With the exception of a few hours when we were carrying the genoa in rather too much wind, making the ship particularly difficult to control, Blondie steered all the time, but because, as I explained earlier, it was not possible to have a vane of sufficient area, the gear was not 100 per cent perfect. But at sea it usually steered well enough for our purpose, i.e. within 10 degrees or so of the set course; we did not strive for greater accuracy, as we had so often found that if we struggle to make southing one day we are probably trying to make northing the next because of a shift of wind; so it is only when we are nearing our objective that we fuss about making good an accurate course.

On a few occasions when we felt it was safe to do so we spent all night in our bunks, leaving the riding light and the radar reflector to keep watch, and oh, what wonderful occasions those were! But for most of the passage we were on or close to recognized shipping routes, and then kept watches day and night, looking out every 10 minutes. In the event we saw surprisingly few ships, but one evening at dusk a Russian freighter, flying an international code signal which we could not understand because when leaving home I had forgotten to bring along the code book, came close and slowed down to leeward of us; we could not read her long name, which was in Russian letters. In good English (we had hoisted our ensign on her approach) she gave us our position by loud-hailer, and as she drew away she made three long blasts on her siren. When we have been at sea for some days, out of all but radio receiving touch with other humans, Susan and I find a kindly action such as this moves us almost to tears. Two evenings later, and at about the same time, we had another visitor. The *Concordia Faro*, nationality unknown, but with a white funnel on which was a black H, came hurrying towards us from over the south-west horizon. She, like the Russian, stopped close under our lee, and through a megaphone her master said:

'I just vanted to make sure you were all right.'

I thanked him and asked where he was bound. We understood him to say 'New York', but this we could scarcely believe because of his approach from a south-westerly direction. However, having wished us good luck, he went ahead, made a turn of more than 90 degrees, and steered west, so we could only suppose that he must have picked us up on his radar a long way off, and then come several miles off course to speak with us.

Our domestic life was simple. We took watches of 2 or 2½ hours, but whoever was on watch had plenty of opportunity to read between visits to the hatchway, and we got ample sleep. I, as is my custom when we are afloat, cooked breakfast, which consisted of boiled or scrambled eggs with toast (with an occasional warm-up and removal of the mildewed outside, the Bermuda bread lasted out the passage) and 'spoon' coffee. Susan did the rest, and lunch was usually hot, canned meat or fish with boiled, sauté, or chipped (depending on the motion) potatoes; and Carr's water biscuits with cheese were popular. But perhaps because of the jerky motion caused by the beam wind, our appetites were never large and our evening meal rarely consisted of more than a cup of soup. For the night watches there was chocolate, and biscuits to nibble and Horlicks to drink. The nights grew noticeably cooler, and we were glad of blankets on our bunks.

Nicholson, who had now been on board for eighteen months,

still did not care much for life at sea, and to our relief rarely went on deck during this trip. But often he sat in the companionway swaying to the motion and glaring angrily at his arch-enemy, the slamming mainsail, until he could endure it no longer and then returned to Susan's bunk or mine, whichever was the warmer, to put in a few more hours of battery charging; however, he woke the moment a flying-fish or squid landed on deck, and, to hell with the mainsail, chased these creatures all over the ship before eating them. Incidentally, we had recently received a letter from Bob Rimington telling us about a visit he and Jay had made during the winter to the Powder Magazine (Nicholson's birthplace) at English Harbour. He wrote:

> 'We had a very pleasant cocktail there, and part of the conversation centered around you and Nicholson. I am glad that he did not take after his mother, whom I regard as a cat of a very low order indeed.'

Susan and I have often wondered just what she can have done to antagonize such a kindly and easy-going man as Bob, and we fear it must have been something pretty bad.

Day followed day, not with regular monotony but with constant interest for us in the ever-changing weather, and in our progress as the miles slipped away astern. During the first week, and in spite of the time spent hove-to, we made good 800 miles, and in the second week 840, leaving only about 130 to go to our destination.

On the morning of our fifteenth day at sea we were bustling along uncomfortably with the wind forward of the beam, and at 0630 the nearest point of Fayal lay by account only 34 miles away, and dead ahead. But the position line obtained by taking a bearing of the radio beacon on Fayal passed 10 miles north of our dead-reckoning position, and as it seemed unlikely because of the overcast sky that it would be possible to get any observations of the sun, I placed my trust in the bearing, and bore away for the island. I should have realized that because of the beacon's geographical position my bearing ran beside high ground and might therefore be in error. Two hours later, when we sighted

Guia, the southern tip of Fayal which we must round to reach the harbour at Horta, it was on the weather bow and we had to come hard on the wind in order to weather it; I realized then that my radio bearing had indeed been wrong, and that I would have done better to rely on my dead reckoning. It was rough going now with the lee deck buried and cascades of spray driving across the fore part of the ship. As we plunged wetly on, watching to see if we were going to pass clear of Guia or not, ahead of us through the haze, which in our experience so often envelopes the Azores and other high islands in similar latitudes, the perfectly proportioned volcanic cone of 7,600-feet O Pico on the neighbouring island slowly took shape—a lovely sight for which one may often have to wait for many days or even weeks.

At noon we weathered Guia and thankfully bore away for Horta, which lies on the island's eastern side, smoothing our water a little then, though it was still quite rough. As we swept towards the port I made the necessary preparations between long looks at the lush, green, mountainsides, for we had seen nothing like this since we left Madeira. I took in the patent log, hoisted the ensign on its staff, and put the Portuguese flag and international code flag 'Q' at the starboard crosstree; I unplugged the navel pipe, hauled out the end of the chain and shackled it to the anchor; got ready the fenders and the dock lines. A local vessel under sail and power, her deck packed with people, came out from behind the high breakwater end as we approached and made her first curtsy to the open sea in a smother of spray, her crew and passengers waving enthusiastically. The pilot boat came out, too, made a circle, and as soon as we reached sheltered water within the breakwater, came neatly alongside without touching us so that the English-speaking pilot (we learnt that he was born on Fayal and had never been away from the island) could step aboard. Surprisingly he remembered our previous visit twelve years before, and greeted us warmly. Susan kept the helm, I started the motor, the pilot

▶

45. Running fast towards the Azores with a deep reef in the mainsail.

10

helped me to stow the sails and then directed us to a berth near *Jomada* (she had left Bermuda some time before us and had taken 18 days) between a pair of clean wooden lighters, which were moored fore-and-aft in the most sheltered corner of the harbour. We took lines to both, and so arranged ourselves that we touched neither, but considerable attention was needed to protect our lines from chafe during our stay, as there was some scend in the harbour and we and our big neighbours surged to and fro. Horta harbour is a busy place, and although the few yachts that call there are made welcome there are no real facilities for them, and as the holding ground is bad they are not encouraged to anchor.

We found the island little changed since our earlier visit, though there are probably now more motor vehicles than ox-drawn carts, and as there is no air-strip it is simple and unspoilt, and the hard-working people just as friendly and courteous as ever they were. The colour-washed town sprawls beside its harbour, into which comes each day a fleet of tuna-fishing vessels, gaily painted, bold of sheer, as well as local boats bringing people and produce from the neighbouring islands, and once a fortnight the graceful old coal-burning steamer *Lima* puts in on her round trip from Lisbon. Above the town, mounting tier upon tier, are neatly hedged fields and market-gardens smelling pleasantly of damp grass and cow dung, and topping a ridge above them stands a row of little windmills, their triangular sails provided with roller reefing gear.

Rua Tenente, which runs uphill beside the harbour, is tree-shaded, its pavements patterned Azorean fashion with designs in black and white cobbles; and half-way along it, squeezed tightly in between the other buildings, is the narrow blue and cream façade of the Café Sport. Here all ocean-voyaging people are given a great reception by Peter Azevedo and his father

◀

46. *Top:* Seen from the Café Sport, the volcanic cone of O Pico thrusts up through a necklace of cloud, a sight for which one might often have to wait for many days. *Bottom:* At Horta the pilot berthed us between two of the lighters which lay moored fore and aft in the most sheltered corner of the harbour. The old coal-burning steamer *Lima* lies at the far end of the breakwater.

in their bottle-lined bar, where the visitor can sit and look out through the doorway across the harbour where his little vessel lies, to the cone of O Pico thrusting nobly up through a necklace of cloud. When we looked in to pick up our mail, Peter at once took Susan into the town, where very little English is spoken, to help her with her marketing, while I, with Jock Hardwicke and his crew Simon, and the people off *Tamuré*, a New Zealand yacht bound for England, sampled the *vinho Verdelho Pico* (a local rosé wine with some of the properties of sherry) and studied the visitors' book in which are particulars of all the yachts that have called at Horta.

We remained in port for five enjoyable days, and as they slipped by we wondered what had become of *Elsie*, and finally guessed that she must have gone on to another island, San Miguel, perhaps. We were not expecting to see *Caravel II*, the trimaran with the Carlisle family aboard, because she had not been due to leave Bermuda until some days after us, but we have never since had any news of her. This, of course, is not surprising, even though her final destination was to have been England, for the British press does not as a rule take much notice of a yacht completing a long trip unless she gets into some sort of trouble, and Britain is too far north for the coconut radio, which in lower latitudes keeps ocean voyagers in touch with one another, to work effectively.

We were only one day out on the trip towards south-west Ireland when we lost the fair wind which had carried us clear of the Azores, and thereafter had calms, one of which lasted for 27 hours, some fog, and light airs for several days, with the result that the passage, which is not much over 1,000 miles, took us 15 days. Often what little wind there was came from ahead, and then we stood away on the starboard tack, as was the practice of the fruit schooners and brigs trading between the Azores and Channel ports when confronted by a headwind, for the farther north one goes the greater should be the chance of picking up a westerly wind. At times we were 60 miles to the north-west of the great-circle course, which optimistically I had drawn on the chart; but this did not benefit us, because, as we were to learn a little later, an anticyclone lay between us and the Channel.

However, after we had been at sea for a week, during which we had sailed less than 500 miles, there were solar and lunar halos, and the barograph, which had been high and steady, began to fall; it dropped steadily one inch in four days, remained there for 12 hours, and then started to fall some more. Clearly something unpleasant was on its way, and gale warnings, which we could now get from the B.B.C. Radio 2, were broadcast for many areas, including Sole, which we were now approaching. The sky was low and heavy, the atmosphere was damp, and an ominous swell rolled in from the north-west.

At noon of the eleventh day, when we still had about 300 miles to go to Mizen Head at the south-west corner of Ireland, the wind at north was so fresh that we hove-to to cook and eat lunch in some degree of comfort; but as the wind continued to increase and the sea grew rougher, we remained hove-to, and several times during the afternoon I went on deck and rolled down more and more of the already deeply reefed mainsail, until by evening only about 75 of its 300 square feet remained set. But at dusk even that small area of sail was too much in a sudden violent screaming rain-laden squall. We dragged on our oilskin suits and went on deck to stow it with some difficulty, Susan working on the windward side of the boom and I to leeward. As soon as the halyard was let go the wet sail beat at our hands and faces, the terylene rattling like machine-gun fire; even to pass tiers round it was difficult, and close though we were to one another I could not hear a word of what Susan was shouting at me. Then with a springy piece of nylon rope we lashed the tiller down, and the ship lay beam on to wind and sea, heeled 15 degrees under her bare mast, and drifting very slowly to leeward. I had taken Blondie's bonnet off some time before, and now we unlaced the weathercloths each side of the cockpit, for if we were to ship heavy water these would probably carry away the stanchions to which they were secured, as they had twice done in the past. Our final act, and no easy one, was to light the riding light and lash it to the boom gallows, where almost immediately it blew out. So throughout the night we had to rely on our feeble electric bow and stern lights; but I doubt that mattered as much as we thought at the time, for heavy rain so reduced visibility that even a bright light could scarcely have been sighted at a sufficient distance to prevent a collision. We wondered, as we thankfully went below, slammed the hatch, and shed our streaming oilskins, how effective a radar reflector really is, especially one carried as ours was only 12 feet above the sea.

Susan managed to heat up the evening soup, and then we lay wedged in our bunks, listening uneasily to the noises of the storm: the whine of wind in the rigging, rising to a shriller note each time we lifted to the top of a sea; the sharp rattle of spray on deck; the angry vibration of the vane on its shaft; the rushing sound of an approaching crest and the shuddering crash as it broke against the weather side. As the night wore on the sea naturally grew rougher, and we shipped heavier crests more frequently. A particularly violent one came thundering aboard at about 0300, and immediately a cascade of water poured down into the galley through the two after ventilators and through the sliding hatch, which the motion had caused to open slightly. At the same time a dollop came in through the water-trap vent over the foot of Susan's bunk and—because of the motion or the angle of the ship at the time—fell on her pillow and head. For a few moments until the ship was able to rid her deck of the burden, she felt buried, heavy and lifeless, and afterwards water sloshed in the slowly draining cockpit well for a long time; eighty strokes of the pump were needed to free the bilge of the water that had entered by way of the cockpit seats, and I had to dress up and go on deck to attend to that job. Nicholson chose the not very suitable time while we were busy mopping up, to take his daily exercise in wild dashes up and down the cabin, with his long thin tail so kinked that its tip almost touched the top of his black head; he then demanded food before turning

▶

47. The town of Horta sprawls beside its harbour, and above it, tier upon tier, are little fields and market gardens smelling pleasantly of damp grass and cow dung.

in on the drier end of Susan's bunk. This, indeed, was a real old night of horror such as we had not experienced for a long time, certainly not on this cruise, and I wished I possessed the tension-free mind of a cat with a full stomach, and could just sleep until it was over. Because of the northing we had made nights were now much shorter, but it did seem a long, long time before the first grey hint of dawn outlined the portholes; we noticed with relief then that the glass was beginning to rise.

We remained lying a-hull for a total of 24 hours. Then the wind backed to the west and moderated, so we unrolled and set some of the mainsail and got moving on our course, and from that time on we had uneventful sailing, though often in mist or rain. But during the forenoon of the day we expected to make our landfall the sun shone brightly and the horizon was clear, enabling us to fix our position with certainty; with a fine west wind to hurry us gaily along, we could not have had better conditions for raising the land, and we sighted Mizen Head in the early afternoon. However, the sky then clouded over again, and as we passed the familiar grey, surf-girt headland, we noticed that a bank of fog was approaching from the westward. If this had overtaken us before we reached the Alderman Rocks at the entrance to Crookhaven (the harbour we were trying for), we would almost certainly have had to stand out to sea and wait for it to clear, for it was too rough for us to attempt to grope our way in blind; but fortunately we just outdistanced the fog to the rocks, and moments later in gloriously smooth water and with the boisterous wind falling light in the lee of the land, we short-tacked gently in to an anchorage off the little grey and white village just as the hills around us grew faint in the rolling fog.

We had chosen Crookhaven as our arrival port not only because it is a perfect harbour easy of access and close to Mizen Head, but because we knew a customs officer was stationed there to attend to the French fishing vessels which put in in connection

◀

48. *Top:* We have often found a solar halo to be a sign of bad weather approaching, and this one was the precursor of a short but violent gale which caught up with us on the way to Ireland. *Bottom:* At rest off the tiny grey and white village of Crookhaven at the end of the Atlantic crossing.

with the lobster fishing. In answer to our signal he soon came off to grant us pratique, and was quickly followed by Perry Greer, a past commodore of the Irish Cruising Club, who came with a gift of real bread—we had tasted nothing like it since leaving Cornwall nearly two years before—creamery butter, eggs which had been laid not in a factory but a farmyard, and milk which had not been fortified, purified, or in any other way tampered with since it left the cow.

Ireland with her kindly, unhurried, soft-spoken people, enchanted us just as she always has, and we were glad we made the detour to cruise there once again for a little while. The Isles of Scilly greeted us with strong spring tides and fog; and as we made our way in rain up the English Channel towards our home port, I suppose it was only natural that we should think and talk a little of the blue and sunny days among the West Indies, and our enjoyment of America's eastern shore, from the spruce and granite of Maine, by the skyscrapers of Manhattan, and along the twisting thread of the Inland Waterway to the palm-shaded Kittredge lagoon. I do hope, though sometimes I doubt this, that we are as kind and friendly to Americans visiting our country as they were to us in theirs.

Once again little *Wanderer* had served us well; she had made good some 15,000 miles on her circuit of the North Atlantic and had called at 250 places. We felt quite miserable when we lowered her flags for the last time and put her up for sale.

INDEX